A CAST IN THE WOODS

A CAST IN THE WOODS

A Story of Fly Fishing, Fracking,
and Floods in the Heart of Trout Country

STEPHEN SAUTNER

Guilford, Connecticut

An imprint of Globe Pequot

Distributed by NATIONAL BOOK NETWORK

Copyright © 2018 Stephen Sautner

Cover and interior photos by Jim Leedom

British Library Cataloguing in Publication Information Available

Library of Congress Cataloging-in-Publication Data

Names: Sautner, Stephen, author.
Title: A cast in the woods : a story of fly fishing, fracking, and floods in the heart of trout country / Stephen Sautner ; foreword by Verlyn Klinkenborg.
Description: Guilford, Connecticut : Lyons Press, [2018] | Includes bibliographical references and index.
Identifiers: LCCN 2018004760 (print) | LCCN 2018007261 (ebook) | ISBN 9781493032099 (Electronic) | ISBN 9781493032082 (cloth : alk. paper)
Subjects: LCSH: Fishing—New York (State)—Catskill Mountains—Anecdotes. | Catskill Mountains (N.Y.)—Anecdotes.
Classification: LCC SH441 (ebook) | LCC SH441 .S27 2018 (print) | DDC 639.2/75709747—dc23
LC record available at https://lccn.loc.gov/2018004760

Contents

CONTENTS

Foreword

Living where I live, I get a good glimpse of the Catskills from time to time. My home is east of the Hudson, and some days the light is so clear that the Catskills, on the western shore, seem to have jumped to my side of the river, especially after snow. Other days, they hunker far, far away, below a lowering midsummer haze, melting into the distance like a neglected burn pile. But no matter how they look, they always seem *other*, darker, more folded, more mysterious than the rational Taconic uplands where I live. I have to remind myself that, once upon a time, I knew the Catskills—knew the river valleys at least—as well as I've known almost any place.

My topo maps of the region—purchased in the early '80s—are thick with penciled reminders of hidden features: the invisible pullout, the productive riffle, the secret rope, tied to a tree near the road, that allowed me to shin down a steep bank to a pool on the main stem of the Delaware, where, in the gloom of astronomical twilight, the mouths of heavy, feeding trout gaped audibly in the dark. On the main stem, I promised myself again and again, to fish all through the night, but I never did because—it sounds pathetic now—I had to go home. I felt the full force of the old maxim—never leave rising trout—but still I had to go home.

It's not that Stephen Sautner decided never to go home again. He does go home from time to time, to New Jersey and to his laudable work with the Wildlife Conservation Society (which is how we first met). But when it comes to the Catskills, he made a very wise decision. Instead of buying a second home there, he bought a first cabin, and a used first cabin at that, with a quarter-mile of its own small stream. How many of us, trudging toward our cars in the darkness with a long drive ahead of us, have dreamed of having just enough cabin to keep the dew off, just enough room for family and a little hospitality? The place I mean is more than merely an oasis in darkness and rain. It's a working laboratory on the banks of the rivers we love to fish, an observatory in the wild. This is the story of that cabin. And like the story of any simple place, it's the story of how not simple that place turned out to be.

I came up to see Sautner's cabin in the spring of 2009 and to spend a night there so I could learn firsthand about fracking. It seemed unimaginable—the fracking, that is. It meant conflict between neighbors. It meant sucking the local rivers dry. It meant injecting a fracking fluid (no one would say quite what it was) underground and fracturing rocks to liberate natural gas. It meant devastation of a kind I'd seen only in Wyoming during the peak of the coalbed methane boom. Stephen, a friend who accompanied me, and I went for a long walk down the neighboring roads, look-ing at potential fracking sites. They were forests, meadows, lawns, clearings, outwashes from former flooding, normal places, places where people would hunt and fish and garden and build cabins. They were also everywhere. And because fracking nearly always implies horizontal drilling, it was almost impossible to say where fracking would *not* occur. The bottom line is this: Every argument used to sell fracking—and the so-called landmen were making a very hard sell—was totally bogus, a lie as basic as Trump's promise to bring back coal.

Sautner talks about fracking and its ultimate political failure in this book, but what he doesn't say much about is the cost of living with the threat of fracking. *A Cast in the Woods* is, of course, a book about a fishing cabin in the Catskills. But it's really a book about the extraordinary couple (never leave Mimi out of the equation!) and their son, who weathered flooding and the threat of fracking and the deeply imaginative decrepitude of a cabin built on rocks with a toilet that flushes to no one used to know where. Fishing in the Catskills can be very hard. It's all the harder when, because of a growing array of environmental threats, you feel an undercurrent of despair in every cast. At times like that, every victory—even a victory over mice, who love cabins as much as humans do—seems like a triumph.

You might, if you've never owned a cabin or an old house, pass lightly over the labor described in these pages. With a kind of gracious nod to the reader, Sautner minimizes how much effort (and I mean effort, not money) he and his family have expended on their cabin. Labor on one's own property is its own gratification, but it's still hard work, whether it's rolling rocks or planting willows or trying to learn enough about the bureaucratic complications of property rights and mining law to stand up to the corporations who would have gutted the Catskill watersheds. In almost everything around him, Sautner finds a spirit of joy, which is all the more remarkable because his daily work—the work that pays the bills—is reporting on the uneven battle between the people who would save the natural world and the people who are destroying it.

Visiting Sautner's cabin reminded me of something I'd learned at great cost 20-some years earlier. I used to drive up to the Beaverkill or the Willowemoc or the Delaware from the Bronx in the early morning. I drove home again the same night, as late as I could stand it. I did it week after week, and I fished without stopping—which means that, most of the time I was fishing, there wasn't a prayer of catching a fish. The sun was too high, the water was too warm, I was standing in the wrong place, I was fishing where there had never been a fish.

But I could work on my casting. I could practice getting a good drift. I could pretend that all my effort to master technique made up for the fact that I almost never caught a fish.

And then one night I fished with Art Lee, who perhaps needs no introduction. We sat in Art and Kris's house and talked and smoked—that is, Art talked and smoked, and I listened. Then, after dinner, we drove a mile or two to a spot by the river and sat while Art smoked a little more. We watched a while. After he saw what he was looking for, Art asked if I'd like to make a cast. I said no because I wanted to watch him fish. He made a single cast, caught a beautiful brown that was invisible to me because it was so unexpectedly near, and released it. And that was enough for the night. This is the kind of thing you can do when you don't have to drive home during those crepuscular hours. And when you're Art Lee—or, I'd add, Stephen Sautner, who will tell me when he reads this that only in his dreams can he fish like Art Lee.

Verlyn Klinkenborg

Introduction

Mutation of an Angler

There is a fishing truism—maybe you've heard it—sometimes called the "evolution of an angler." It goes like this: First you want to catch *a* fish—*any* fish—regardless of species, size, or technique. As long as it has fins, it's fair game. Traditionally this has meant bluegills, worms, bobbers, snelled hooks, old Zebco push-button reels, or even cane poles. But it could also be the first time you tentatively waded into a river, clutching a fly rod rigged with a Hare's Ear Nymph.

After that brief moment of glory, when your bobber (or strike indicator) slips under and your prize is brought to hand, you very quickly advance to the second level: the desire to catch *a lot* of fish. Depending on where you like to go fishing, this could mean more bluegills or maybe a mess of bullheads or a limit of stocked trout or, in coastal areas, perhaps a sack of mackerel or a pail of snapper bluefish—basically any species where you can catch 'em by the bucket or fill a stringer or gluttonously catch and release until you lose count.

The next phase is *big* fish—you know, slobs, pigs, or simply "large." Many anglers' evolutionary progression dead-ends here, and they obsessively while away their remaining fishing careers, slinging eels for 50-pound stripers, or they double-haul 2/0 mouse flies at midnight for leg-sized brown trout or swim enormous live baits for largemouth bass that could swallow a volleyball.

If you manage to evolve beyond that, you want *hard* fish. Here's where fly fishing on chalk streams using size 26 midge pupae on 8X tippet comes into play. Or the machoism (is it masochism?) of fishing for muskies or Atlantic salmon or some other "fish of a thousand casts."

Then finally, the last rung on the evolutionary ladder is reached: catching fish *on your own terms*. This last phase is subject to widely varying interpretation. For some, it might mean slow-trolling traditional hand-tied smelt patterns for landlocked salmon—but only from a restored birch bark canoe after ice-out in Maine. Or it could be a regression to bluegills and cane poles— but this time with kids or grandkids.

For me, this pinnacle of angling evolution, this summit from which I would loftily make Zen-like, mindful casts, was this: I would buy a place—a fish camp—in the trout-filled Catskill Mountains and fish whenever the hell I felt like it.

The idea seemed so simple: a cabin so I can fish more. Spend less time driving and more time fishing. Get to know a few streams really, really well. Become a "sharpie"—the 10 percent of the anglers who catch 90 percent of the fish. Saunter around with a content, fish-induced glaze.

Damn, if only it was that easy.

It turns out that actually owning a fishing cabin, as I have since 2003 near the Upper Delaware River, has morphed—some might say mutated—into something far beyond fishing. For me it's become an unending quest to preserve "Dark Hollow," as my friend calls the place because of its shaded, deep-woods setting, to keep it exactly as I first perceived it: pristine and pure, even though I've come to realize that this vision is pure fallacy.

Conservationists sometimes talk about "shifting baseline syndrome," the perception that what's unspoiled or untouched is often in the eye of the beholder, and it changes with each new generation—usually for the worse. Think of bison, for example. Visit Yellowstone National Park today, and all seems well; thousands of animals graze upon rolling hills. They look abundant and happy. But ask a Shoshone about the current state of bison, and you might get a slightly different opinion.

Sadly, I have experienced shifting baselines myself with fish I grew up catching in my home state of New Jersey. Take whiting—a saltwater fish once known to swim so aggressively into the surf chasing baitfish that they would actually beach themselves on cold winter nights. Old-timers called it frost fishing, and they would describe filling bushel baskets with the delicious silvery fish. By the time I started seriously surfcasting, whiting were in decline, and I was too late to experience true frost fishing firsthand. But you could still catch whiting from boats offshore, which I did—just before the stocks finally collapsed due to overfishing and climate change. Nowadays, I would have about as much chance of fishing a run of whiting in the surf as I would seeing a flock of passenger pigeons roost in the Catskills as they once did by the tens of millions. Anglers who came up after me have probably never even seen a whiting and therefore will never miss them like I still do.

Some of this shifting is obviously inevitable. Changes to the climate are already being felt, and like it or not, they will alter things like weather patterns, forest composition, and some wildlife migrations. But by God, I am not going to be the one to sit idly by while the native trout in the little stream that runs past the cabin wink out because a flood washed away the shade trees that keep it cool. Nor will I allow the woods to be taken over by invasive Japanese knotweed or my favorite hard maples stripped by forest tent caterpillars or the landscape run roughshod by natural gas fracking—at least if I can help it. Nor will I allow mice to sneak into the cabin and get in my wife's hair.

Oops. Getting ahead of myself.

So my baseline is this: a simple cabin on 14 acres of wildlife-filled woods and a quarter-mile of native trout stream. A half-dozen other great trout rivers a short drive away. Family and friends who stay there with me. Neighbors whom I have gotten to know so well over the years. Moments of incredible beauty and wonder, with notable encounters with various birds, frogs, snakes, salamanders, bears, mayflies, moths, and other critters.

And of course, fish; I have gotten to understand the inner workings of a six-foot-wide trout brook more than most anglers ever will. And sloshing through this stream in a bathing suit in the summer with my son, Finn, beginning when he could walk, catching everything from frogs to crayfish, has been one of the great joys of owning the place. Meanwhile, the Upper Delaware and other Catskill rivers have served as an Angler's Institute for Higher Learning. There I have honed my skills catching wild brown and rainbow trout, along with American shad, smallmouth bass, and walleye.

Anyone who has taken a biology class remembers that mutation is a key part of evolution. You know, drop a tail here, grow an extra toe there. Sometimes it works out for the best. Darwin's finches come to mind. Other times it doesn't, like the story I just read on the internet about a turtle born with two heads on a reptile farm in China.

So has it worked out for me, an angler who bought a cabin to fish—and only fish—but wound up hopelessly intertwined in something much larger than merely fishing? Have I become a graceful finch with a highly specialized bill or a two-headed turtle lumbering aimlessly in circles? I leave that up to you to decide.

Perfection

In May 2004, I stood on the deck of a floating house anchored in a side channel some ten miles south of the main-stem Amazon River. A several-day meeting of Amazonian experts and various conservationists had just ended, and some of us had gathered outside to relax before a riverboat would eventually take us downriver to the Brazilian port city of Tefé.

It was the high-water season, and the river swirled and surged, running the color of coffee with just a splash of milk. Clumps of fallen tree branches, palm fronds, and other leafy debris had accumulated on the up-current side of the house and had begun to rot in the tropical sun, giving the air an earthy, fertile smell that was not unpleasant. On the far side of the channel, pink river dolphins, called botos, would occasionally surface with a breathy swoosh. Behind the floating house, in the vast, seasonally flooded forest known as the *várzea*, a troop of black howler monkeys called in the distance, their raspy sounds reminiscent of holding a seashell to one's ear. Overhead, raucous shrieks of macaws pierced the air, their electric blue and red plumage flashing like an exclamation point.

Below me, in the dark water, untold numbers of fish swam past. Eight-foot-long pirarucu—a giant predator that looks curiously like an enormous guppy—would sometimes surface to gulp air. Shoals of piranha lived under the house and would skeletonize our table scraps whenever we scraped them into the river. On the

bottom, unseen, lurked literally hundreds of other species: mostly various catfish but also electric eels and freshwater stingrays.

With the Amazon pouring its heart out that afternoon, it should have been a moment of entrancement or at least blissful observation of the natural world humming along in fifth gear. Instead, I remained distracted. You see there was this cabin in the Catskill Mountains some 3,200 hundred miles to the north . . .

On the overnight flight home from Manaus to Newark Airport, thoughts of the cabin continued. It had been nine months since my wife, Mimi, and I bought it as a weekend retreat/ fishing camp. Since then, we had spent most of our Saturdays and Sundays working on it—mostly cleaning, scraping, painting, and setting it up. Now for the past week, while I remained tethered to the floating house on the Amazon, a local contractor had been working on the biggest job to date: transforming the outside.

For decades, the exterior of the cabin had been covered with sheets of asphalt made to look like bricks. But they were strange looking: extra thin with pastel shades and odd geometry. There are still a few old sheds and barns nearby with the same siding.

The theory is that a local salesman made the rounds in the area decades ago and did well for himself.

To cover these odd faux brick walls, we chose rough-cut, or Adirondack, siding—whole logs unceremoniously ripped into boards at a sawmill. Wavy edges, uneven ends, saw marks, bark, and knots are their hallmark. Many consider it junk wood, but it can be beautiful, rustic stuff. We chose hemlock: rot-resistant due to its high resin content; native; and, most importantly, inexpensive. Just before I left on my trip, a truck delivered the planks from the local sawmill and left them on wooden pallets stacked all around the cabin.

Mimi picked me up from the airport, and we headed directly upstate. She had stayed at the cabin earlier in the week while the contractor and his assistant worked. She said they did their job slowly and thoughtfully, like they were assembling a giant puzzle. She told me they would nail up a plank, consider it for a long minute often while smoking a cigarette, then search through the stack for just the right piece to match it with. They both told her they had never worked with Adirondack siding before and were enjoying the challenge.

"Well, how does it look?" I repeatedly asked. But she just smiled as we continued driving.

The foliage started to change the farther north we drove. Though I was gone only a week, it already felt and looked like summer when I landed. Most of the trees had fully leafed out, and the grass had turned a deep green, less so the more we drove. I watched May slip back into early April. Fully developed leaves shrunk into mere buds. Cherries, crabapples, and eastern redbuds that had already dropped their flowers nearly a month ago blossomed once again. By the time we made the last turn down the long hill that leads to the cabin, there was little more than a warm, chartreuse glow around most of the hardwoods.

We dropped into the valley. We drove past a field scattered with dairy cows, then we passed my neighbor's family farm—three houses of various sizes, a barn, assorted sheds, and a pond. We slowed and made a hard right off the road into what looked like just woods but was really a hidden grass driveway. It led over a short rise past three mature Norway spruce trees on the left that stood one after another like immense guarding soldiers. Their long sweeping bows gave the effect of a tunnel as we drove beneath them. To the right was a steep, ferny hillside. A mix of hemlocks and hardwoods provided additional shade. We parked, shut off the car, and got out.

There, in a clearing stood the cabin, resurrected. The new hemlock planks, now the color of honey but soon to be stained dark, ran horizontally along its length. The carpenters had clearly built well. Where one plank ended, a new one of virtually the same width joined it, and the course continued. The siding was framed by sturdy two-by-eights that ran lengthwise along each of the cabin's four corners. The windows were similarly framed. The waviness of the hemlock's edges, the knotholes, and the bark made it look like the entire structure rose from the woods themselves, which in a way, it did.

As I gazed at this new center of the universe, other things came into focus, too. The brook chuckled away, mere feet from the cabin's screened front porch, which was strategically and safely perched on a high bank. The brook ran clear and bank-full. Its stony bottom had begun to take on a warm, golden springtime color, already shedding the sometimes-blackish algae that grows in the winter. I knew some early mayflies—mostly blue quills and some Hendricksons—had already started hatching along with the first of the caddis and that native brook trout and a scattering of rainbows that lived there would pounce on virtually anything that floated. And I knew my six-and-a-half-foot two-weight—the perfect fly rod for the little stream—was already rigged with a bushy Adams, and it hung invitingly on two hooks on the front porch.

I followed the brook upstream with my eyes, noting some of the trout lies I had learned over the past nine months: the undercut bank beneath the three birches where you could often watch brookies rise to midges; the surprisingly deep plunge pool below the submerged table-sized river rock worn smooth; and the Shipwreck Pool—named for the five-foot-long jagged stone that looked like the hull of a capsized schooner. The first rainbow I ever caught in the stream came from there—a plump seven-incher that jumped repeatedly before I released it. Mature hemlocks, ash, river birch, and a scattering of planted spruce lined the streambanks. Their foliage kept the stream shaded and cold, while their mesh of roots kept banks from slumping. Farther upstream, the brook vanished in the darkness of a steep, wooded ravine. Downstream, it would eventually join the Delaware, one of many nearby Catskill rivers known for large wild trout.

The woods themselves smelled of dew and new growth. Shafts of sunlight spiderwebbed through the evergreens and speckled the ground. Fiddleheads had begun to unroll, and a few burgundy trillium flowers could be seen here and there giving dots of color to the otherwise somber early spring undergrowth.

Overhead, the first wave of warblers and other spring migrants sang. A phoebe, repeating its wheezy trill, looked for a perch to construct its nest of moss and mud. The repetitive "*here I am, over here*" of a red-eyed vireo had begun and would continue unendingly until the middle of July or later. The rhythmic, almost Latin song of a black-throated green warbler buzzed high in the canopy—a musical proclamation that it had safely returned from wintering grounds in Central America or Mexico. And all the while, a chorus of hundreds of spring peepers called loudly from a wet hill on the other side of the road.

Deeper in the woods there were other unseen animals, too. Black bears whose tracks and scat I sometimes saw while hiking; white-tailed deer that last fall gathered each morning under an apple tree in the yard; and even a bobcat I once glimpsed just a few yards from our fire pit before it vaulted across the stream and bounded up a steep hillside into thick unbroken forest. Lesser creatures, too: wood frogs, spring salamanders, red-spotted newts, luna moth larvae, and glowworms would all soon emerge from their respective winter beds of bottomlands, leaf litter, and fallen logs.

I continued to watch and listen, breathing in lungfuls of silky May air. Here was the North American version of the Amazon, these great eastern woods. And our cabin high above a trout stream would be our own version of a floating house to observe nature humming along in fifth gear.

I took in another deep breath, turned to Mimi, and uttered these fateful words: "It's perfect."

The Search

The seed to buy a cabin was first sown several years earlier while on a fishing/camping trip along the Upper Delaware River. I knew a certain island—now posted, sadly—that boasted a lovely campsite known only by a few trout fishermen and canoeists. A friend had let me in on the spot but told me not to tell anyone. Because the Upper Delaware—widely considered the best wild trout fishing east of the Mississippi—was nearly three hours from my home in suburban New Jersey, overnight stays were mandatory unless you wanted to stumble blearily through your front door in the wee hours.

The campsite was a secret worth keeping. It sat on a high bank and boasted a sweeping view of the river. Enormous white pine trees towered over it, keeping it shady and cool. A century of fallen needles made for luxurious, soft bedding to pitch a tent and unroll a pad and sleeping bag. Other amenities included a picnic table dragged there by some unknown benefactor and a well-constructed fire pit ringed by flat rocks—perfect for resting pots and cooking implements. There would always be some kindling and a few logs left behind as a courtesy for the next camper. You were expected to do the same, and we always did.

On a warm, humid June day during trout season, Mimi and I beached our canoe in the backwater behind the island and set up a pleasant camp. After dinner, we fished in the run immediately downstream of the island. At first, fish rose sporadically.

But the main event took place at dark, when we were treated to a dense spinner fall of brown drakes—a relatively rare hatch on the Delaware that lasts only a few evenings. Trout came up greedily, sipping and gulping down the meaty mayflies literally just off our rod tips. But it turned out to be one of those times when spinners blanketed the water, and the trout were nearly impossible to fool. It was still fun just to witness such an impressive hatch, and we continued fishing until we could only hear the sucks and slurps of unseen trout gorging in the darkness. After fishing, we hung up our waders, stoked up the campfire, and poured ourselves a night-cap. Eventually we went to bed in sultry, almost summery air. A gentle breeze blew, and the sound of whispering pines overhead competed with the gentle hiss of the river. Sleep came easily.

At around midnight, I awoke to the first rumble of thunder. It sounded far away. Then I saw a faint flash of lighting through the tent, followed by another low, rolling grumble. A distant, late-spring thunderstorm coasted along somewhere in the river valley well south of us. I sighed contentedly, feeling particularly snug in our tent.

But slowly the thunder grew louder and the lightning brighter. The sound of the pines overhead turned raspier, until they eventually drowned out the pleasant din of the river. Soon after, I could hear raindrops hitting the rainfly of the tent. The storm seemed determined to muscle its way up the river valley. And my God, did it.

The lighting became more and more intense. It would illuminate the inside of the tent every few seconds, followed by increasingly louder claps of thunder. I thought Mimi had been sleeping until, on a particularly dazzling flash, I saw her staring at me saucer-eyed. A second later, an absolute howitzer blast of thunder sprung both of us upright from our sleeping bags. With the next burst of lightning, we looked at each other helplessly.

With a full-blown squall now raging overhead, it suddenly occurred to me that the once-delightful towering white pines that shaded us earlier in the day now loomed over us like menacing ogres—or better yet lighting rods. I was convinced it was only a matter of time before one of them would get struck, sending down a half-ton limb that would squash us like two ants. Or we would simply get electrocuted outright.

The storm seemed to stall directly above us. Lightning was so close you could hear the sharp crack of electricity just before another percussion bomb defibrillated our chests. Rain poured down. I remember looking at my watch: one o'clock; then two o'clock; then, sometime later, fitful sleep.

Morning. We unzipped the tent and crawled outside into thick, leaden air. Everything that was not in the tent or under a tarp was soaked. Our waders, left draped over branches, had since fallen and were now partially filled with rainwater. I looked at the canoe and could see a forgotten roll of toilet paper swollen and floating in six inches of bilge.

We reorganized the camp as best we could. I drained the canoe, and we laid out gear to dry on the picnic table. Then I fruitlessly tried to make coffee over a campfire using soaking-wet kindling. And it was at that very moment the kernel was planted: "Maybe," I thought, "just maybe, a cabin might be better than this."

A cabin! We could have fished until late, then retired to four solid walls and an even more solid roof. We would have had a few pleasant after-dinner drinks and maybe some dessert while we sat on a screened porch. I'd be in slippers. Mimi would be reading a book. Then we'd cheer on the storm under warm and dry blankets. And, most importantly, I would be drinking hot coffee right now instead of hyperventilating into a pile of wet twigs and watching a slug crawl up my empty cup.

But then the fire crackled to life. Coffee was made, and the cabin-seed went dormant for a few more years. The long-range fishing trips continued to the Delaware and other far-flung rivers. It always seemed like the best ones—the West Branch, the Neversink, the Beaverkill—were the farthest away. We'd fish until late, followed by the inevitable long drive home while trying to stay awake; or we'd camp or occasionally splurge for a motel room.

As sometimes happens in life, it took a tragedy to finally motivate—in this case September 11, 2001. Suddenly there was an urgency to get things done in one's life—particularly things that involved being far away from New York City in case the big one went down. And so the search began in earnest.

I looked at hundreds of listings on real estate agents' websites. Phrases like "country charmer" and "woodsy retreat" seemed to be endlessly repeated, but usually, they were neither charming nor woodsy. There were entire mountains for sale (complete with your own stone quarry!), palatial riverfront trophy houses with a runway for your plane, split-level homes straight out of a Long Island suburb, working dairy farms, and double-wide trailers. But there were surprisingly few true cabins in the woods—at least the kind we were hoping to find.

Then came appointments with various real estate agents. We would explain how we were looking for just a simple cabin, and they would nod knowingly and tell us they had just the place. But it turned out their ideas and ours were wildly divergent.

One of the first properties we were shown featured a house built of cinderblocks that could have doubled as a bomb shelter. It had few windows and felt chilled—like a good place to age meat. Surrounding it was a five-acre lawn that looked like it would take an entire weekend to mow. "No," we explained. "We're looking for more like a cabin, something woodsy, you know?"

"Oh, I've got just the place," said the real estate agent. The next property he showed us was literally a ten-by-ten wooden shed no more than 30 yards from a working railroad. Inside, the furniture consisted of two cots shoved against opposing walls. The "kitchen" was a camp stove on a metal folding table in the corner. No running water, electricity, or bathroom. He told us a couple of hard-core deer hunters owned it, and we believed him.

We actually considered it. Maybe it would be just like a sturdier version of a tent. And an occasional old rumbling freight train might be fun in a hobo, Boxcar Willie kind of way. Maybe I'd learn to play the harmonica. But more importantly, the property had another amenity: a couple of acres of actual Delaware River frontage literally on the other side of the tracks. So we hiked down a brushy trail leading to the river to survey the fishing possibilities. A slow-looking run flowed past—not great trout water but perhaps a decent place to fish for smallmouth or shad, or maybe it would be a nice swimming hole in the summer. But on the hike back we found a deal breaker—actually several—crawling up our legs. Wood ticks. I had seven; Mimi had an even half-dozen. Not sure how many the real estate agent had. Indiana Jones hates snakes; Mimi hates ticks. Next listing, please.

Real estate agents may have begun to tire of us—me especially. There was one cabin a fairly long drive from the agent's office, but it seemed to have all of the boxes ticked off: rustic yet charming—owned by an artist—and hidden down a long gravel driveway shaded by beautiful, mature maple trees. But when we got out of the car, I took two steps, stopped cold, and told the real estate agent to forget it. "Why?" he asked.

Beyond the maples, maybe a quarter-mile up a nearby hillside, I could hear the roar of a state highway. There was no way, I explained, I could commune in the woods listening for warblers and thrushes over the sound of Jake-braking Peterbilts. He may have stopped calling after that.

Another real estate agent told us this time he really, truly had just the place. "A real *cabin*," he assured us. So he took us down a pleasant wooded dirt road that lurched abruptly to the right, then headed nearly straight up what could best be described as a medium-sized mountain. "Might need four-wheel drive to get up here," he told us while downshifting into lower and lower gears. "So the first home improvement," I thought, "would be to buy a Jeep."

But then the road ended at a small but sturdy wooden cabin with a truly spectacular river view. And it was quiet up there. Things began to look up. Then he unlocked the front door, and we stepped inside. It was small, just one room with a loft but with a nice porch with that same incredible view.

The cabin itself was dark, with few windows. And then we both saw the painting. It hung dead center on the largest wall—clearly there as a centerpiece. It sort of reminded me of a Native American symbol, the one that looks like a swastika. But the truly creepy part was that the symbol was made up of strangely contorted women's legs complete with fishnet stockings and high heels.

The real estate agent must have saw us staring, so he said, "Cabin's owned by a New York City detective. He likes to paint, too." Somehow this did not make us feel better. I began to think his inspiration must have been some horrible crime scene. We umm-ed and err-ed until I changed the subject by asking where the bathroom was, as I didn't immediately see one.

"Bathroom? You bet," the real estate agent said cheerily. "Just outside, follow the rope." And sure enough, tied to a rail on the porch, was a long rope that led along the edge of what looked like a cliff and ended at what I assume was an outhouse. I say assume because I never looked inside to confirm. Clearly, late night toilet visits would have a downright expeditionary feel to them. So we politely said we would think about it but already knew we would be passing on the severed-leg Nazi cabin.

Time passed. Later that summer, we came close to actually buying a decent A-frame near the Beaverkill River but lost to another bid at the last minute. This wound up probably being a good thing, as the cabin only had a generator for electricity. Hauling up gallons of gasoline in the back of our car to run the refrigerator would have gotten old over time.

Over the fall, I continued to look at more online listings but found nothing new unless I wanted to buy a 500-acre beef-cattle farm with good land for logging or a lakefront contemporary complete with media room for a cool half-million.

So perhaps it was out of desperation when we decided to drive upstate once more to check out a double-wide I saw listed. At least the location looked nice—a few acres of woods and close to the Delaware. So we drove up on a bitterly cold Saturday in early January and met the real estate agent in his office. Then we drove a few miles out of town and turned up a rutted driveway, where, on a concrete slab, the home sat, sagging slightly amidships.

There was a truck parked in the driveway. A guy in his late 20s answered the door. He looked like he just woke up but said we were welcome to look around. If he straightened the place up a bit for the real estate agent and his clients, he had not done a good job. Clothes, dirty dishes, and other ephemera laid scattered about. The agent opened the bedroom door, and we saw a pile of blankets on an unmade bed. Then the blankets began to move, and from underneath, a pair of feet poked out, complete with red toenail polish.

"You know," I said as politely as possible while backing toward the front door. "I think we're good. Thank you so much."

Back at his office, the real estate agent explained that— clearly—we would be buying that property just for the land.

Then we would have the doublewide hauled away (he knew a guy), and we could build our own dream home right on the site and move right in. I nodded and may have grunted a little just to be polite.

I glanced around at some of the other listings taped to the walls. Then I saw one that I remembered from the website. It had a silly title: "All That and a Bag of Chips!!" The listing described a two-bedroom cabin, including a separate bunkhouse, located on a small stream with 12 acres of land. But in the pictures, the cabin looked odd and sort of homely with this strange brick exterior.

Not wanting to have wasted another three-hour drive, I half-heartedly asked, "What about this one?"

The real estate agent looked up at the listing and said, "Oh, that. It's actually off the market for now. The sellers may list it again this spring. But if you want to drive by and take a look, I'll tell you where it is."

He drew a quick map and sent us on our way. We drove along a quiet paved road that paralleled an unfamiliar but beautiful stretch of the Delaware. There were deep azure pools and broad trouty riffles. I kept stealing glances while trying to keep my eyes on the winding road.

After a few miles, the road made a hard right away from the river and turned to dirt. We continued to follow it. It now paralleled a small stream and wound its way slowly up a hill. Trees seemed to close in while the stream played peek-a-boo, passing back and forth under the road a few times. There were no houses in sight and in fact no signs of humanity except for the road itself.

Eventually we came to a fork, and directly ahead, through a row of mature spruce trees, we saw the cabin for the first time. It sat across the stream, nestled in the snow on a little hill. Though it stood only 100 feet from the road, it was surprisingly hidden in a mix of hardwoods and conifers. It looked unoccupied; no driveway had been plowed, and the windows were dark. We pulled to the side of the road and stepped into the cold. The land laid nearly silent except for the muffled gurgle of the brook running between snowdrifts and a lone chickadee calling in a spruce tree above us.

We didn't say anything to each other at this point. Almost instinctively, we both scaled the snowbank along the road then made our way closer. The snow was nearly waist deep, so we trudged along slowly, Mimi following my path. As we approached, I could see that the strange brick siding was actually just rolls of asphalt that covered what appeared to be a classic one-story wood-frame cabin. It was about 20 by 30 feet, with a long porch running along the side facing the stream. The porch was screened and closed in with jalousie windows.

We reached the closest window, shielded our eyes from the outside glare, and peered into the main room. I couldn't see much—a knotty pine wall, a woodstove, and a table. All I could hear was our own breathing and the low rush of the stream maybe 30 feet away. That was enough.

Then I turned to Mimi, who was already looking at me knowingly. This, absolutely, was the place.

We looked around for just another minute or two and then practically raced back to the car. We flew back down the dirt road and sped along the river—glancing at trout pools, of course—then we burst into the real estate agent's office, breathless.

"That's the place," we declared triumphantly, pointing at the listing on the wall and then back in the direction from where we just came. "That's definitely the place."

But instead of dancing around with us in celebration, the real estate agent seemed nonchalant, bordering on indifference. "Well, like I said, it's not on the market right now. But I think the sellers will list it again in the spring. Give me your name and number, and I will call you."

"Yes. Please. Call. Please. Yes," I said over and over, writing down my name and phone number in big, easy-to-read block letters. Then we drove three hours home.

I waited a day or two but then decided to take matters into my own hands.

The real estate agent had mentioned the seller's last name in passing when I first asked about the property. And although I couldn't remember it fully, I did at least recall the first letter. That was enough for me to begin my detective work. I called the town clerk that afternoon and sheepishly asked if she could help me track down the name and address of a property owner in town. I was fully expecting her to say that I would have to come there in person or put my request in writing or some other bureaucratic obstacle that I surely would have faced back home in New Jersey. But not in rural, upstate New York on what must have been a very slow Tuesday afternoon in January. Instead the clerk said, "Why *sure*, hon, let me see if I can help you. What's the first letter of the name again, and what road is it on?"

Then she slowly and methodically went through names one by one and cross-checked them with addresses until she finally found the name of the owners and where they lived. It turned out they were from New Jersey, too. She then gave me their full name and mailing address all nice and slow until I had it all written down. I don't remember the town clerk's name; Madge sounds right. In any case, I thanked Madge profusely—I would have kissed her if I was there in person—and hung up.

Then I began to write a letter. But this couldn't be just any letter. It would have to be the kind where you were sincere but not shy about tugging on some emotional heartstrings if need be. The kind of letter where you get one shot to plead your case. The kind of letter that all your future hopes and dreams rest on. So I wrote. I wrote about beauty, nature, family, tradition, happiness, and of course fish and birds. And I might have thrown in puppies and kittens, God and country, too. When I mailed it, I knew I left it all on the field, so to speak. Then I waited.

A week or so later, I received an e-mail from the owner's son. It read:

My mother asked me to respond to the letter you sent to her on January 22nd. The cabin was for sale, but it looks as though a contract will be executed in the next few days. Our childhood memories are of the years of weekend road trips in the family station wagon looking for a "place." My dad finally settled on "the cabin" in the early '60s and spent as much time as possible there. He said that he "lived for the place and could not imagine his life without it." My parents always said that if we wanted a house he would stay home. It became a special place with wonderful memories for all the family. My father passed away a year ago, and my mother recently decided it was time to sell. The place is just too closely associated with my dad for us, and it is impossible to not just think of him, to miss him, when we are there. A little cabin in the woods with a picturesque stream, native trout, great hemlocks, magical tree roots, ferns, and rocks. A fairy land for young children and young at heart. I hope that you find a place as special to you as this was to my dad because I suspect that you are kindred spirits.

I tried reading the letter out loud to Mimi but couldn't finish. So she read it herself and looked up at me teary-eyed. My God, talk about leaving it on the field.

But, wait—a contract? Executed in a few days? After a quick discussion with Mimi, I decided in a blur of keystrokes to outbid whomever was about to steal *our* little cabin in the woods—the one with a picturesque stream, magical tree roots, ferns, and rocks. An hour or so later, I received a phone call from the seller's son, Joe, who wrote the letter. He explained that he had taken the cabin off the market last fall after some sort of spat with the real estate agent about an unlocked door that wound up blowing open. Since then, a work colleague found out about the place and made a cash offer that the family was about to accept. So I made our counteroffer over the phone in between reaffirming my love of ferns and brook trout. There was a pause. Joe suggested we meet him the following weekend. He said we should actually look inside the place to make sure we knew what we were getting into before he accepted our bid.

So the next weekend, we drove up again. This time I brought along my older brother, Gene. He is fluent in the language of Guys-Who-Can-Fix-Stuff, in case the conversation with the seller devolved from trout and hemlocks to plumbing and wiring ("Two hundred; two twenty-one; whatever it takes"). And he would also know what to look for in case the cabin was about to collapse from termites or ants. I, on the other hand, could be standing waist-deep in termite sawdust oohing and aahing at the perfect nook to set up my fly-tying table. Gene, who I should point out doesn't fish, brought along a single tool—an awl, which he would use to strategically poke at wood like a dentist looking for a rotten tooth.

We met Joe on the road in front of the cabin. He was in his early 50s and soft-spoken. He brought along a friend, and we all trudged through the still-deep snow and made our way onto the porch, where we stomped off our boots and breathed smoke. I glanced out the jalousie windows, saw the stream a short cast away, and had a sudden premonition of sitting in an Adirondack chair, sipping a beer while looking at a trout rise. Then Joe undid a combination lock on the front door, and we walked inside. It was cold in there and dark, and my eyes had to adjust from the brightness outside. The inside admittedly looked a little tired, but it still had lots of potential. Meanwhile, Mimi just stood there grinning and looking everywhere. This was her blank canvas. She had been squirreling away furnishings, artifacts, and other items since we began our search a year and a half ago. Now she was imagining exactly where everything would go.

Except for one wall of knotty pine, the main room was covered in old paneling. But it was roughly installed, with uneven gaps on the bottom and no floor molding to cover them. There was a small connecting kitchen and a tiny adjacent bathroom that contained a pink toilet, blue tub, and peach sink.

Two doors led to respective bedrooms. The larger one had its own sink, which seemed like an odd luxury, and flowery wallpaper covered one of the walls. The smaller bedroom was more basic, with a raw-plywood ceiling. The most prominent feature in the main room was an enormous Franklin stove with gold trim that was supposed to be installed into a wall but instead stood nearly in the center of the room.

Joe explained that most of the furnishings and decorations were throwaways from friends' or family member's houses or items they just happened to find. He pointed to the large kitchen sink that had a 1950s industrial look to it and told us it came from an old Dairy Queen.

Then he said, "Whenever we were thinking about really fixing the place up, my dad would always remind us: it's a *cabin*."

Mimi and I both nodded, and Joe seemed to let those words sink in. Looking back, I believe he said that for our own benefit.

He told us more about the history of the place. It was built in the 1940s as a primitive one-room hunting camp. The bedrooms and bathroom were eventually added. The porch was expanded and screened in after an incident with his mom and a bat that he didn't elaborate on. As he spoke, there was a tinge of sadness in his voice. I imagined that seeing the family cabin cold and largely empty—and now about to be sold—was not easy. The more I looked around, I could see small details that told the history of the place—the dozen nails hammered above a doorway with a turkey feather stuck in one of them (someone's hunting scorecard?) and the old retired trout spinner hanging from a shelf with a broken hook—what had it caught?

Then Joe told us about the other prospective buyers. He said they were a recently retired couple who planned on moving some-where down south but still wanted a place "in the mountains" for the summer. Then he said that he didn't think the wife actually liked the place and that the husband mentioned that they might tear it down and build something new on the property. Mimi and

I could tell Joe did not like the idea of their family cabin being demolished, so we reassured him that was not our intention at all, that we were looking for a cabin just like this one, and now we had found it.

We eventually went outside to continue our tour. Twenty feet from the cabin itself, there was a separate outbuilding with a sliding glass door. Joe explained that it was originally used as a separate bunkhouse for kids and guests. More recently, his brother, an artist who worked in metals, had requisitioned it to store some of his raw materials. We peered inside and could see it was filled with scraps of iron and strange, heavy-duty tools.

We walked back to the road, then hiked along it for a quarter-mile until it came to the end of the property line. The stream ran parallel for the most part, though it sometimes looped away through the woods before joining us again. I saw a few early brown stoneflies crawling around on the snow, which prompted me to ask about the fishing. It turned out Joe wasn't much of an angler, but he said other members of his family caught plenty of trout—mostly natives but occasionally some "nice rainbows" that ran up from the Delaware. At that point, drool may have been collecting in the corner of my mouth. The idea of *owning* a quarter-mile of my own private trout stream, even one that was just six feet wide, sounded like heaven. On the other side of the stream was a steep, densely forested hillside. Joe explained that the property line continued for another quarter-mile into those dark and mysterious woods.

We eventually headed back to our cars and stood for a while and talked. "Now that you've seen it, are you still interested?" Joe asked.

I looked at my brother who had been discretely poking around with his awl since we got there. He nodded and confirmed in his best Guy-Speak, "It's in good shape."

So we told him yes, then we shook hands all round, and headed home. We signed a contract the following week.

But as much as I was hoping to move into the cabin by early spring, it was not to happen. The main delay was due to a land survey, which the bank required for a mortgage. It turned out there had never been one before. So that meant hiring a local surveyor, who of course was backed up with other jobs. He finally began working midspring but then hit delay after delay. Joe had warned me about local contractors, explaining that they work hard but do so at their own pace. He recommended I stay in close contact with the surveyor and gently nudge him, or it could wind up taking a long time.

So I called every once in a while to see how things were going. Each time there would be another reason for the survey not being completed. One time he told me there was a hold-up because it had been raining.

I said to him—and I was honestly not trying to be the snarky city guy—"Don't you just wear raingear?"

"It's not that easy," he assured me.

Spring turned to summer, and politeness turned to anger—probably fueled by already missing the best fishing of the season. One day in July, I called and screamed into the phone, "It's been six months! What is taking you so long? Do I have to yell to get you to finish the survey?"

A week later, not only was it completed, but the surveyor also had found an extra acre and a half of land. Maybe I should yell more often.

Then finally, in early August, we gathered in a local bank and signed paper after paper and form after form. Joe and his mom weren't there—only their lawyer. Then, when the last form was signed, we were handed two sets of keys. We left the bank, and with a car full of various furnishings, a cooler of food, some sleeping bags, and a few fly rods, we drove at long last to our cabin in the woods. We eventually turned into the grass driveway and past the three spruce trees and the ferny hillside and parked.

The cabin was ours.

Now what?

Fixing, Upping

As much as I wanted to immediately string up my two-weight and ravenously fish the stream for the first time, we instead took stock of what was in the cabin and what we would need to make it a fish camp. A few weeks earlier, as we neared the final stage of closing, Joe mentioned some furniture he would leave behind if we wanted it. This included a kitchen table and a bed, along with two chairs and a small couch on the porch. When we unlocked the door and walked inside, it turned out only the porch furniture still remained. Whether his siblings had changed their minds about certain items or the communication didn't make it to whomever actually did the moving, it meant we would sleep on an air mattress on the floor that first night. It was like camping all over again—minus the fear of electrocution.

But there were other things left behind we hadn't discussed. The kitchen was stacked—literally—with metal storage lockers filled with service for a small army. Dozens and dozens of plates, bowls, cups, and glasses were crammed inside each locker as if the cabin could sleep 50 instead of maybe five very, very close friends. Joe did mention he came from a big family and that his mom spent most of her time cooking, so I guess that explained it.

So we sorted and sorted. We kept a set of six space-age coffee mugs straight from the set of *I Dream of Jeannie* and some drinking glasses that looked just like the ones my mother used when I was in third grade ("More Hawaiian Punch, Stephen?"). The

rest we brought home and eventually donated. Other items we decided not to touch. The aforementioned nails and turkey feather and the old trout spinner remained where they were left, along with a set of keys hanging from a nail that didn't seem to work in any door. We found a small plastic sign hanging in the kitchen called "Indian prayer." It said not to judge a person until you have "walked a mile in his moccasins." Another sign hung from the front porch door that read, "Peace to all Who Enter Here." It seemed like good karma to keep these things in place, so we did.

We began to liquidate and replace other items. The enormous gold-trimmed Franklin stove that looked like it could double as an iron forge wound up in a friend's deer camp. We replaced it with a 100-year-old cast-iron beauty that my brother rescued from the curb on a local junk day. He had the removable boot warmers replated with nickel (he knew a guy), then he wire-brushed off the rust, and repainted it black before presenting it as a cabin-warming gift. It incinerates logs with incredible efficiency and roars loudly when fully stoked and vented. Narrow the vents, and it burns slowly, giving off great waves of warmth while cast iron crackles and groans. In early spring and fall and on cold mornings regardless of the season, it is the very heart of the cabin. And it functions nicely as the proverbial 19th hole—a place to gather after a cold, wet fishing trip.

We replaced the avocado-colored oven that looked like it could roast four turkeys at once with a relatively tiny apartment stove—one of the few new appliances we have ever bought for the place. The "autumn harvest"–colored workhorse refrigerator—another '60s museum piece—hung on a little longer until it began to make strange noises and we received an electric bill for almost $200. I got rid of that one myself, dismantling the door and hauling the beast out on a hand-truck to a waiting pick-up, then finally chucking it in the town dump. The second new appliance, an equally diminutive apartment refrigerator, now stands in its place.

Then came weekends of removing old wallpaper, followed by lots of painting. The kitchen came first; we peeled the walls and ceiling (yes, ceiling paper), then painted and stained. The bedrooms followed. It turned out that the strange white-with-blue-grain wood paneling accepted two coats of sage-green paint nicely, making the bedrooms look warm and woodsy.

Except for the one knotty pine wall, which we didn't touch, we painted the entire main room brownish red (or is it reddish brown?). This took more than one attempt when, after our first try, it looked creepily like we had covered the place in blood (maybe a good color for a certain cabin on top of a mountain). It was at this point I began to notice that, whenever we walked into the local paint and hardware store, the owners were grinning.

After we finished painting, our attention turned downward to the floors, where linoleum seemed to cover every square inch. The porch featured a 1960s confetti pattern perfect for the kitchen of a swinging bachelor pad. The rest of the cabin had the exact same red-brick design from my parents' kitchen circa 1976 (must have been a sale at Sears). All were peeling and cracking and showing their age. The porch turned out to be an easy fix. We took utility knives to the confetti and hauled it out by the bagful to the dump. The rough wooden floors underneath had been painted primer gray. We painted them a sort of chocolate brown.

When I pulled up the linoleum in the main room using a snow shovel, I found a subfloor underneath made from a type of particle board. Back at home, I began pricing traditional wide-planked floors that looked perfect for the inside of the cabin. The ones I liked best were reclaimed from an old barn and made of oak. They looked worn and weathered and had saw marks from when they were first cut. But with that provenance came a price—not cheap.

The next weekend, I stared at the subfloor again and considered my options. Maybe we would have to go with those press-on fake wooden floors—practical and relatively cheap but not in the spirit of a fishing cabin. As a last resort, I took out my utility knife and cut a small piece from the corner just to see what was underneath. A warm golden brown glowed back. I excitedly made a larger cut, lifted, and behold: Wide-planked oak floors gleamed like riches from Tutankhamen's tomb! And yes, they were worn and weathered, with saw marks from when they were first cut. I celebrated—for five minutes. For as great a discovery as this was, removing the rest of the subfloor proved to be an arduous task. Whomever originally installed it must have really despised those wide-planked floors. There were literally hundreds and hundreds of carpet nails that needed to be pulled out one at a time. For the next few days, instead of waders and a fly rod, kneepads, a pry bar, and a hammer would occupy most of my free time. The sound of hammering, punctuated by me swearing and cursing, drowned out the chuckle of the stream. The floors in the bedrooms turned out to be wide hemlock planks that looked as if they were installed last week. We stained and sealed them.

Let's not forget the bathroom. Well, maybe we should. We looked at the mismatched sink, the toilet, and the tub and considered it for a minute or two. Everything worked: The toilet flushed, the sink turned on and off, and the shower was hot. So we shut the door. Remember, as Joe rightfully pointed out, it's a *cabin*. We did get a new shower curtain and I believe some soap.

Over at the bunkhouse, the rusting iron artifacts were long gone, presumably removed by Joe's artist brother. It now stood as just an empty ten-by-ten square room. The dark paneling on its walls, again slapped up and mismatched, somehow went with the general feng shui of what a bunkhouse should be, so we didn't touch it.

All along we filled our car each weekend with beds, chairs, tables, rocking chairs, a futon, cots for the bunkhouse, canoes, a kayak, and of course more and more tackle and fly-tying supplies. Slowly our fishing cabin was taking shape.

At this point, with the various walls, floors, ceilings, major appliances, and basic furnishings largely in order, there was a division of labor. I turned my attention to the outside, while Mimi began to "set up" the inside.

I took on the fire pit as my first order of business. If the woodstove represents the very soul of the inside of the cabin, the fire pit can claim equal billing outside. Ours was already sited in a decent spot—close to the stream and a few short yards from the bunkhouse. But it seemed to just be some sort of rusting piece of circular metal shaped like a giant inverted hubcap. In fact, it looked like it might not be a fire pit at all but rather just a place to burn garbage.

So I removed all doubt. First, the hubcap went to the dump. Second, I invited over my fishing buddy Jim, an engineer by training but with an artisan-woodsman's sensibility. He and I began rolling large rocks from the woods or hauling them up from the stream. After a few hours, we had assembled a fine—I dare say lavish—fire pit. It was circled with large, thick rocks, wide and flat, with lots of room for everything from a full-size cast-iron skillet to a 12-cup camp coffeepot. A few feet from the pit, Jim assembled three stone benches. Two were single-seaters, but the other could fit two adults or three kids comfortably thanks to a four-by-two-foot perfectly cut bluestone slab we found near the shed. We decided to situate it facing the stream. It may have been destined for someone's rustic doorstep, but it now found a permanent home as a fine perch to both fire-gaze and stream-gaze at the same time.

I quickly learned that there was no shortage of rocks. They laid scattered in the woods; outcroppings jutted from the ground, and the stream when it ran low sometimes looked like a small quarry. This provided an endless supply of building materials and inspired my next project. The cabin has no foundation; it sits on pilings made of concrete-filled drums sunken into the ground. So I decided to construct a rock wall in the one- to two-foot gap between the bottom frame of the cabin and the ground. The previous owners had put up a small wooden garden fence around the base of the cabin—probably to keep critters from venturing underneath. But it looked like it had seen better days, so I dismantled it and tossed it into the fire pit. Then came more rolling of rocks and stacking them into a low stone wall. I quickly learned to avoid "running joints"—repeated gaps in successive courses of stone that can lead to a weak wall that can topple. A half-ton of rocks later, it was done, and I had entered into the millennia-old fraternity of Guys Who Build Walls with Rocks. Now, whenever I look at the low-slung sturdy wall, a primitive, druid-like itch feels thoroughly scratched.

But the abundance of stone was not always welcome. When I tried to dig some holes to transplant a few ferns to the front of the cabin, I could barely go an inch before thudding into yet another rock. It seemed as though the entire property sat on one enormous stony pile with a little dirt wedged between gaps. But the ferns were eventually planted, and they somehow flourished even in such a paucity of decent soil.

Meanwhile, Mimi looked like a frantic squirrel building its nest. Every time I saw her, she hurried more boxes and bags and other items into the cabin. Then came noises of hammering things to walls or the low groan of furniture moving about. I could already see rooms starting to transform, but whenever I wanted to poke around for a closer look, she would say, "Not yet."

Then she finally announced, "It's ready," and showed me onto the porch. The green from the beech trees, just a few feet away from the open jalousie windows, gave the room a treehouse effect. The gentle rush of the stream filled the room with white noise. A few threadbare oriental throw rugs—finds from secondhand stores—softened the wooden floors. To the immediate right, the left-behind couch sat. I quickly learned that, if you sit on the right-hand side, you have a clear view of the pool directly in front of the porch. And if you look long enough, you can see the wink of a brook trout rising in the knee-deep slot against the far bank. If there is a better place to sip a morning coffee or an evening beer, please tell me, so I can go there immediately.

Past the couch, the two original porch chairs faced away from the stream toward the inside of the cabin. Beyond them the fly-tying desk—also with a stream view—occupied the far corner. A vintage creel with a built-in aluminum tackle box etched with the original owner's name hung from the wall to the immediate right. On the other side stood a narrow bookcase, the top shelf crammed with field guides—everything from birds to spiders to mushrooms. I have since filled the bottom shelves with dog-eared angling classics, such as Sparse Gray Hackle's *Fishless Days, Angling Nights*, arguably my all-time favorite fishing book. It chronicles the so-called golden age of Catskill fishing from the 1940s and 1950s, when it seemed like all anglers wore fedoras and thoughtfully smoked pipes between casts. Joining Sparse is the more obscure *The Sweet of the Year* by Ray Palmer Baker Jr., a beautifully written ode to springtime trout angling that simply must be reread every April. And then there's *The Wedding Gift*, the oddly named book by 1930s and '40s Hollywood screenwriter John Taintor Foote about a fly-fishing obsessive who drags his wife to a remote Maine fishing camp for their honeymoon. Please note that similarities to me are purely coincidental, and besides, we went to Alaska on our honeymoon and fished for salmon. Few how-to fishing books are found on these shelves, especially when you can walk right out the front door and learn pretty much whatever you need 30 feet away in a rushing watery classroom. And on the center beam that runs the length of the porch, my trusty two-weight fly rod rested on two pegs, my own version of the proverbial shotgun above the mantle.

Artwork and artifacts competed for your attention. Small framed trout portraits hung in strategic places. A vintage net dangled from the center beam. A wooden fish decoy lurked on a shelf under a small table. Keeping with Joe's cabin theme, most furnishings and decorations were secondhand: either castoffs from friends or ferreted from junk shops. Yet it all fit.

Across from the fly-tying desk was the upright futon—admittedly a new purchase but worth describing, as it may be the best place on the planet for an afternoon nap, either pre- or post-fishing, and especially true when serenaded by vireos or the waterthrush that claims the stream as its own from May through early July. On warm nights, the unfolded futon has become the bed of choice, with the stream serving as the perfect noise machine. Turn out the light—maybe after re-reading Sparse Gray Hackle's *The Lotus Eaters*—and watch utter blackness envelop the room. Then, slowly, as eyes adjust, the faint silhouettes of trees can be seen. On full moons, silvery shadows dapple through the canopy. Sleep here comes quickly and deeply.

It was time to walk inside the main room: Peace to All Who Enter Here. Amen. There, the woodstove stood at attention awaiting further orders. An old rocking chair served as a fire tender's seat, where one could safely feed the stove without getting singed. To the left, against the wall, was the bottom half of an old hutch with crackled paint and beadboard doors. It now functions as a sort of bar, and visitors instinctively set up their various libations there. Hanging on the wall above this happy place was a framed print of a hickory shad by S. F. Denton, commissioned by the state of New York in 1895 to document all of its varied gamefish. Two other prints hung in the room: an old Audubon of a wild turkey and an original folk-art oil painting of a bugling elk done lovingly by someone who clearly knew more about elk than painting. It cost five dollars in a junk store. Next to the light switch hung a small wall calendar from a coal delivery service from 1955. That cost a quarter.

Speaking of bars, the taxidermist who stuffed the chain pickerel staring down above the entrance to the kitchen may have had one too many when he painted it. Its namesake chain pattern looked more like curly spaghetti, but it's an otherwise fine skin mount. Another fish has since joined it: an ancient cutthroat trout that came from a fishing cabin in Montana. A friend gave it to me after his wife redecorated their den and said enough is enough. One new piece of furniture we bought functions as a sort of booth that sits in the corner of the main room. It serves as a kitchen table, dining room table, card table, and a cold-weather fly-tying desk when the porch is frigid and the woodstove is roaring.

The kitchen, tight as a galley on a submarine, had to be well-planned to take advantage of every possible morsel of space. We replaced the metal lockers with an enameled metal cupboard on rollers, with a wooden cabinet stacked on top that served as the pantry. Thankfully it just fit between the refrigerator and the Dairy Queen sink. Various metal bread boxes sat on shelves, protecting everything from oatmeal to coffee from potential critters.

Speaking of coffee, back home my morning routine is little more than flipping a switch on an electric pot and walking away. Not so at the cabin. First, I pour beans into a wall-mounted manual grinder. The grinding serves as an alarm clock to all fellow coffee drinkers. The grounds collect in a detachable glass cup.

Then I fill the pot—a battered metal percolator with a glass top that looks like it came from a caboose. I have to watch the proverbial kettle boil (yes, it eventually does) and immediately turn it down to a simmer, or it will spit all over the stove. For the next ten minutes, while the coffee gently percolates, I may wander outside to see what songbirds are calling or check on the stream. By the time I come back into the cabin, the smell of brewing coffee has fully permeated. Then I grab one of the *I Dream of Jeannie* mugs, pour in some milk, then settle on the couch on the porch, where I might spy a brookie between sips. Want a cup?

And the bathroom—well, you already know about that. Did I mention we bought soap?

Next were the two bedrooms—both set up to be dark and quiet. Overnight guests often sleep surprisingly late in them, wandering out in the morning, saying, "Is it *really* 10:00?" Perhaps it's the mountain air or the sound of the stream. The smaller room featured a small display of fishing artifacts—among them a Bass-O-Reno, a Flatfish, and a trout leader case that looks like an aluminum hockey puck. A late friend's favorite Adirondack pack basket hung from a hook (and it always will). A display of large and impressive sphinx moths, collected and pinned by Jim (also an amateur entomologist), sat in a shadow box. A single bookshelf contained a few Zane Gray novels along with some overflow from the porch fishing library, including Ray Bergman's *Just Fishing*, first published in 1932. But the most prominent feature was a large framed promotional poster for the London and Northeastern Railways about commercially trapping eels, which presumably you can see—not do—from the comfort of the train. That bedroom is now known as the "Eel Room"—a name that causes some overnight guests to flinch when initially told they will be sleeping there.

The slightly larger bedroom was set up with late-night reading in mind. A vast collection of mysteries—mostly Dorothy Sayers, Agatha Christie, and P. D. James—lined the shelves. I guess sometimes there's more to solve than just what's hatching on the stream.

Finally, the bunkhouse. Two cots lined with feather beds and topped with light wool blankets rested against each wall. Another threadbare oriental rug lay between them. On the wall above each cot hung a Denton print: on the left, the fallfish—much maligned but actually one of the few native predators in the Upper Delaware. On the right, the more glamorous striped bass, which occasionally strays this far upriver. A calendar from 1962 called *Canadian Gamefish Parade* with Kodachrome images of everything from smallmouth bass to Atlantic salmon hung on another wall. Two ancient steamer trunks rested at the foot of each cot. They store everything from extra camp chairs to tents. Hanging from nails on various crossbeams were old oil lanterns, a retired canoe paddle, and a clear bucket used to collect and observe aquatic insects. Above it all, the skin mount of a five-pound walleye stared down with crazy eyes. Hence the bunkhouse's eventual name, the "Walleye Room."

When fishing buddies come to the cabin, most of them invariably want to stay in the Walleye Room. They drop their kit bags and proclaim, "I'm sleeping here!" It does have the feeling of an old-time clubhouse—a place to hang your slingshot and check your pockets for frogs before you turn in.

So that's the nickel tour. Time to fish.

April 27: The stream is high, stained, and cold—but still fishable. With drizzle falling and temperatures in the 50s, I opt for chest waders—normally overkill here, where a deep pool is barely up to your knees. But today I welcome the extra layer of waterproofing.

I re-tie my leader for the first time this season. The 4X tippet from last year has four wind-knots in it—probably from casting giant attractors that twirl the line. Yet I continued to make carefree casts with it for most of last summer and into the fall—testimony that a break-off from a fish is virtually unheard of here and that this is not the place for precision tackle.

I continue to play it fast and loose by selecting a Brown Bivisible—an ancient pattern rarely used anymore. It was tied by my late friend Richard Kress. I choose it for two reasons. First, Rich's flies catch fish. Two years ago, on the Delaware, his March Browns vacuumed up big trout better than a gillnet. Secondly, like the Bivisible's name implies, you can see it—particularly the white collar of hackle at the forward end. Even in the froth and bubbles of today's high flow, I should be able to track it easily.

I wade into the stream and already can see a few Hendrickson spinners buzzing around. A good sign—fish should be looking up. The air is peppered with the smell of wet woods, and I take in deep, nourishing breaths as I begin casting. The first few casts go ignored, but then at the tail-out of a flat, a trout rises up, tracks the fly for a second, and then returns to its lie. A second cast is made, and it comes back for another look. On the next cast, the fish tentatively nibbles at the hackle before darting away. It doesn't come back. It might have been four inches long. Probably a rainbow—too fast for a brookie.

The next pool—the prime undercut directly in front of the cabin— is too fast in the higher flows for a good drift. I make two quick casts anyway before moving past it. The pool after that is a four-foot-long watery chute of slightly deeper water. I put the fly at the head, and a fish immediately rises up and takes it down. It is hooked, and I bring it to my hand. Again, a rainbow, maybe five inches—a fish born in the stream last year. It will remain here for the summer, grow another inch or two, and then drop back to the big river. Right now in my hand, it is a scale model of one of the 18-inch screamers I sometimes catch in the Delaware.

After I release it, I cherry-pick some of the better pools and a few promising runs and pockets. A few more tentative looks at flies from small fish—including a very bold brook trout that looked to be no more than two inches long. Some of the other more reliable pockets are too high to get a good drift.

The drizzle stops, and the sun comes out, sending shafts of sun-light shooting through the hemlocks and dappling the stream bottom. Finally, I reach the last pool right at the top of the property line. It is worth the wait. It may be the one legitimate trout pool of the entire stretch—fully 20 feet long and nearly waist deep—at least in these higher flows. In the summer, my son and his friends hike here and then dare each other to dunk underneath the always-chilly, shaded, spring-fed water.

A slab of bedrock runs along the right bank, and a deep scour adja-cent to it often holds the best fish in the pool. I cast the Bivisible there and watch as it floats through a good-looking bubble line. Nothing rises, so I let it drift the full length of the pool just in case something is holding right at the lip. Still nothing. I cast a few more times with the same result. But I know there's a nice trout in the pool. There has to be. That is, unless an otter or great blue heron beat me to it.

Then I remember a fly on my dry patch from a previous fishing trip—a weighted, chartreuse Mop Fly. It's as ugly as it is utilitar-ian—little more than a "micro-chenille" fiber cut from a hand mop and lashed to a hook with a small gold bead at the head. It resembles nothing in nature—at least nothing I have ever seen—but some anglers swear by it. A few weeks earlier, I used it to fool a few hatchery rainbows on a stream in New Jersey. But those were fish raised on pel-lets and only stocked a few days earlier. A far cry from a wild, stream-bred trout—one that's had to eke out a living on aquatic insects, some unlucky ants and beetles, and maybe an occasional darter—all while dodging everything from whirligigs to kingfishers. But the fly will get down deep and that's where the trout must be holding. So I tie it on and make an awkward cast with the little two-weight.

The fly plops in at the head of the pool. I let it settle for a few seconds, then feel a sharp pluck. I lift the rod but fail to connect. A sub-merged branch? I cast again. The fly settles. Another pluck. This time I lift and briefly feel weight, followed by nothing. So I cast a third time and then watch as a large brook trout tracks the fly all the way to the tail of the pool before snapping at it. I lift and this time pull the fly right out of the fish's mouth. The trout holds for a few moments, perhaps five feet away from me, before easing back to deeper water. On any other stream, this fish would have bolted under the nearest rock after the first missed hook set, let alone the third. But not here. These mountain trout have a special sort of innocence, or maybe it's just plain hunger in otherwise stingy waters. So on cast number four, I feel a hard take, and the trout is solidly hooked. It thrashes on the surface, and I can see that it will actually need to be played rather than craned in, Huck Finn style. It blows out of the pool into the next run, but that's the end of the show. A few seconds later, it is in my hand. It's a full nine inches long and small-headed—a female. It has the regulation full brook trout regalia, which I admire for a few seconds—especially the red spots haloed in blue, which seem so unnecessary on a trout and yet so very welcome on my eyes. I release the fish, knowing it will probably be the largest brookie I will catch in the stream all season. But that's OK.

I wander back to the cabin along the wooded ridge that parallels the stream. I walk slowly along dodging orange newts clambering in the wet leaf litter and notice for the first time the red-eyed vireo that's been calling all the while in the trees above me.

The Biggest Smallest Stream

I am an angler, not a golfer, so my advance apologies to all you duffers whose passion for the game I do not share. Don't get me wrong: I can understand golf's appeal—sort of. The satisfaction of a 300-yard drive might feel like double-hauling 100 feet of fly line. Though I wouldn't really know because I've never done either (God knows I've attempted the latter—many times). But in the end, I still side with Mark Twain, who notoriously called the sport a "good walk spoiled." Like I said: my apologies.

But miniature golf—now you're talking. No hole more than 20 feet away. The challenge of putting under the turning blades of a mechanical windmill. The precise ricochet off a side bumper, followed by a slow roll into the cup. And of course, there's the always-challenging 18th hole, where you can win a free game if you manage a hole in one.

And this might be why it was love at first sight between me and the six-foot-wide stream that ran past the cabin. Here was a place where I could take everything I knew about fly fishing on your regulation Catskill trout river and render it to a simple roux: reduce the five-weight rod to a two-weight; cut back a 12-foot leader by six feet; substitute chest waders with knee-high rubber boots or, better yet, shorts and wading sandals. The six fly boxes in my vest became six flies total, and even that was often five flies too many. In fact, I shed the vest completely. A pair of nippers and some forceps pinned to a shirt or jacket, and I was ready to cast.

Ironically, the one thing that did not shrink was the size of the flies I used, which in fact grew larger. I quickly learned that this was not a stream for size 22 Sulfur Emergers and PhD trout. Here, a size 12 Adams or size 10 Stimulator or Turk's Tarantula was king.

And that elusive 100-foot double-haul? Forget it. Here, a long cast was 15 feet. If I had to strip off an extra arm's length of line for a farther cast, the sound of the ratcheting reel startled me. Most pools were the size of a bathtub, some half as big. Some holding lies could fit inside a shoebox. No drivers here, no five iron to get the ball from the fairway to the green; everything was a gentle putt. The overhanging branch became the windmill; boulders became bumpers from which to bounce the fly into a pool or likely run. And, deliciously, the free games were unlimited. Yes, I fell deeply in love.

All told, the stream is about three miles long from its source to where it enters the Delaware. It originates from a wet meadow lying in a saddle between two mountains. I hiked there once with my neighbor Tim. We made our way up a series of old hunting trails and eventually crossed into a tract of state-owned forest that Tim said hadn't been logged in perhaps a century. And it showed. As soon as we entered the state land, trees seemed to double in size. There were black cherries—choice lumber around here—more than three feet across. Tim showed me a truly giant hemlock that to me looked as big as a redwood. I took a picture of it and later sent it to a friend who is a state forester. He speculated it could be as much as 700 years old. Beyond the trees, we could see the meadow—four or five acres of tall grasses ringed by more forest land. It looked like it once was a beaver pond that had shallowed out over time. I walked to the edge and could hear the gentle purl of water running from somewhere beneath the grass.

After the stream leaves the meadow, it gathers several more tributaries—little more than narrow rills tumbling through clefts in the forest. Eventually it enters a ten-acre natural pond. Tim told me the pond once was the source of ice for local farmers. They would saw off thick slabs, haul them into their cellars, and cover them with straw for insulation. They would last through the summer.

Once the stream exits the pond, a dirt road follows it all the way to the Delaware. The first mile of that stretch—between the pond and my property line—I know mostly by walking or driving alongside it. At the pond's outlet, it runs past some houses before entering a heavily shaded gorge. Then it quickly drops from pool to pool until it eventually plunges over a 20-foot waterfall. I've never fished above the falls nor in the ten-acre pond. I'm sure there are trout in the stream but probably not in the pond itself, which has been stocked with largemouth bass. Trout are rarely found with bass, unless you count inside their stomachs.

A half-mile past the waterfall, my home water begins. At first the dirt road is literally a cast away, but then the stream tumbles off to the left behind a stand of hemlocks, birches, and maples. Several springs recharge it here, and a dense forest canopy keeps it cool. Then it flows past the cabin itself and through a culvert pipe, where it leaves my property. Fully half of my quarter-mile stretch is not readily visible from the road except for maybe a glimpse or two through the trees. And that's how I like it.

In this water there are brook trout and rainbows—all wild. How big do they get? Before I answer, let us first consider the sliding scale on the handy gamefish ruler, which goes something like this: a 1,000-pound blue marlin is a 50-pound striper is a 35-pound Atlantic salmon is a ten-pound largemouth bass is a four-pound brook trout. But of course, you need to factor in things like location and the size of the water you are fishing, not to mention technique. Ergo, a four-pound brookie caught in Labrador might actually just be an average fish, while in Maine, it would make front page of the *Bangor Daily News*. Head farther south, and that four-pound brookie gets less and less likely, so the scale needs to adjust. Here in the Catskills, any wild brook trout over a foot is noteworthy, though a fish caught in still water, like a beaver pond, could tape out to 14 or even 15 inches. Use the sliding scale to add an inch or two if it was caught on a dry fly (12 inches on a dry is the same as 14 inches on a streamer, etc.). So, taking all of the above into account, the fish in my stream are . . . small. How small? Figure your average trout is between five and six inches. Anything over seven is noteworthy; nine inches is a trophy. The largest trout I've ever landed in the stream is a ten-inch male brook trout with a long snout I caught in late September. It was so jazzed up in prespawn colors that it reminded me of a Christmas tree, complete with blinking lights. On the other end of the scale, I have somehow caught trout barely two inches long—usually fingerling rainbows. How they managed to even wrap their tiny mouths around a hook remains a mystery. But make no mistake, these diminutive wild trout in this headwater stream can still be the object of obsession every bit as much as their larger, more celebrated brethren downstream in the Delaware. I speak from experience.

The first trout I ever caught in the stream, I documented in a journal. All I wrote was "August 2nd, 1st brook trout—seven inches." And though I don't remember the exact details of that catch, I can say this with certainty: It rose to a dry fly, took no more than ten seconds to land, and was an extraordinarily beautiful fish, with a mix of yellow spotting and a scattering of fine-tipped red spots haloed in white and blue. A butter-yellow worm track ran over a blueish-olive back. I know this because all of the brookies in the stream are like that: stunning and suckers for anything that floats.

The wild rainbows in the stream are the progeny of spawners that run up from the Delaware sometime in early April. I am amazed that they somehow can navigate to my stretch of river, leaping past a series of narrow three-foot-tall waterfalls and a poorly placed culvert set too high off the streambed. Yet they manage to leap these obstacles every year, as evidenced by the fingerlings I see zipping around in the shallows in June. These fish will live in the stream for a year or so, growing to six, seven, or maybe eight inches. Then they eventually head downstream and enter the banquet hall otherwise known as the Delaware River and its famous hatches-on-steroids. There they grow very large and strong. The brookies, on the other hand, are content to live their entire lives in the stream.

I have seen actual spawners from the Delaware only a handful of times. Once in April, I spotted a pair of 14-inch rainbows paired up in the tail-out of a pool a half-mile below my property. The next morning they were gone, but I could see the nest they cut in the gravel and even a few neon-orange eggs scattered about. And then there was the large rainbow I hooked briefly in the undercut bank directly in front of the cabin in early May one year. The stream was high that season, so the fish must have lingered longer than usual. It might have been 16 inches long, and when I spotted it, it looked as out of place as a bull elephant trying to hide behind a sapling. It actually rose to a dry but shook off after a second, then casually cruised into an undercut bank. It never came back and was gone the following week. Yes, it would have been the biggest fish by far I ever landed in the stream, and no, I still don't want to talk about it.

I've seen brookies spawning just once, in late October, in water so shallow their backs were showing. But for the most part, spawning for both species takes place either too early or too late in the season for me to witness it.

As for brown trout, I have only caught one in the stream, though they are abundant (and large) in the nearby Delaware. The fish I caught measured a full six inches, and I took it in one of the relatively deep pools upstream of the cabin. My theory is that spawning browns can't or won't jump the culvert and the falls, but evidently at least one pair got up the courage at some point and made the leap(s).

In terms of other fish, I have caught a few darters and sculpins in aquarium nets and have seen schools of black-nosed dace pushing water in some of the flatter pools. There are no suckers or fallfish, at least in my stretch of stream. They, too, are probably thwarted by the falls and pesky culvert. But there was a relatively giant fish that once lived briefly in the Shipwreck Pool. It was late September, and I was casting my way upstream, when I saw something large holding in the slot next to the pool's namesake rock. It looked to be easily 18 inches long and three inches across. "A spawner!" I thought, thinking a big brown trout, which spawn in the fall, had finally jumped the culvert and navigated the falls. So I cast to it a few times, but it wouldn't take. Then I decided to slowly approach it so I could at least catch a glimpse before it spooked. That's when I saw a jagged black lateral line running down its flank and an enormous Edward G. Robinson mouth. A largemouth bass. As I got closer, I could see that it looked gaunt—maybe only two pounds (it should have been three if it was healthy). And it was banged up, with scales missing. I stared at it for a few seconds trying to consider how the hell it got there. Then I realized that it must have come from the pond upstream. That meant it swam—or more likely washed over—the 20-foot waterfall and then pinballed through various pockets and chutes until it wound up in the pool in front of me. Not wanting a convalescing largemouth nursing itself back to health by eating trout like popcorn, I got Mimi, who stood at the tail of the pool with a landing net. The fish literally had nowhere to run, so chasing it downstream into the waiting net wound up being fairly easy. After that, we put it in a bucket and walked up the road to Tim's dad's farm pond and dumped it in. I presume it lived out its remaining days preying on more appropriate bass food like frogs and bluegills—not wild trout.

I've never conducted rigorous aquatic insect surveys in the stream where you key out certain anatomical details to identify the scientific names of every critter living under every rock (too much Latinizing), but over the years I have catalogued a surprising abundance of insect life. Definitely not as much as the bug-factory Delaware but enough that certain rocks, particularly those in the oxygen-rich riffles, seem to be crawling with critters. These include many of the requisite mayflies, caddis, and stoneflies found in the big river. But there are few true "hatches" in the classic sense, with flotillas of duns riding the current and trout rising everywhere. And many heralded Delaware bugs—like the silt-loving green and brown drakes—are missing altogether because the rocky, rushing stream is virtually silt free.

In terms of traditional, seasonal insect emergences, there are a few blue quills and a decent amount of Hendricksons. And though I only see the duns trickle off here and there, I do sometimes see small clouds of spinners gathering above certain pools in late April and early May. Next come sulfurs, and there seem to be many species that hatch beginning in May and lasting throughout the summer. I gauge their abundance by the number of bugs hanging around my porch light. On some evenings in June, there can be as many as a dozen, which is about as prolific as the hatch seems to get. Isonychias, whose free-swimming maroon-colored nymphs are like candy to Delaware rainbows, start to gather around the porch light in June and continue into October. The elegant, white-legged spinner—called a white-gloved howdy by the old-timers—reminds me of a bug dressed up for a night on the town, which in a way it is. Ubiquitous blue-winged olive mayflies live here, too, and can show up anytime between April and October.

Sprinkled throughout the season are various caddis flies ranging from the teeny-tiny black caddis to the relatively giant yellowish-orange sedge caddis of September that spans nearly a full inch long. Then come my favorites of the stream: the stone-flies, particularly the golden stone. These clumsy 747-sized fliers are a turkey dinner with all the trimmings for a trout. I believe most of the time that, when a fish comes up and takes a whack at a large dry, regardless of the pattern, it thinks it's a stonefly. The nymphs are fascinating. A few times a year, I arm my son and a few other kids with aquarium nets and a clear plastic bucket and flip rocks in the stream to see what we can find. Stonefly nymphs, which are nearly always the largest bug in the haul, are surefire crowd-pleasers. Flat but striped like a hornet they look as if they should sting or at least bite, but they are completely harmless. Stick your hand in the clear bucket, and they will inevitably cling to it trying to find shelter between your fingers, which tickles. Eventually, the nymphs crawl out of the river and up trees or whatever else they can find, split their exoskeleton, and then hatch into winged adults. We find the husks everywhere, including on the cabin. If we find a particularly large husk—some are a full two inches—we immediately attach them to our shirts like some ento-mological insignia. Yes, my family is a bunch of proud bug geeks.

On the other hand, whatever you do, don't mess with a hell-grammite, the fearsome larvae of the massive dobsonfly with jaws that look like they could double as a bottle opener. The big ones span more than three inches long and have centipede-like legs they use as leverage to wrap their bodies around your finger like a boa constrictor. Occasionally they will come up in our bug hauls, where they immediately prompt squeals and shrieks. Some of the kids find them scary, too.

Other assorted critters I have found in the stream include craggy dragonfly larvae; crayfish; frogs; pollywogs; and a few species of salamander, ranging from the diminutive two-lined to the extremely impressive spring salamander, which can measure nearly nine inches long. They live up to their name—all the ones I have found have been within a few feet of one of the springs that enter the stream. They prey on other salamanders, and I've read that they in turn are relished by brook trout. May I someday meet the brookie that can take on one of these beasts.

Back to the fishing. As I mentioned, the dry fly rules here. I can count on one hand the number of fish I have taken on a nymph or streamer. If the water is too cold for trout to come up to a dry—usually either very early or very late in the season—I will go birding or, God forbid, find some chores to do.

Over the years of angling on this tiny stream, I have developed a technique that to the casual observer might look like a really bad golfer hacking away at a ball stuck in a sand trap. I cast *a lot*. I am constantly peppering the stream with minicasts every which way as I make my way along from pool to pool. Conversely, sometimes on the Delaware, I may go 20 minutes between casts waiting out some brute that sucked down a single March brown, then apparently decided to take a nap before its next trip to the surface.

Not here. The trout hold in precise lies: the saucer-sized eddy behind the boulder, the slightly deeper scour next to the bank. And there are a lot of potential lies, so I cover each of them with multiple casts. Often a fish may miss or flash behind a fly. If so, I cast again and then again. Sometimes I check the rod high and dap the fly, twitching it to get the fish to finally commit. Often the magic number is three: On the first cast, a trout may move briefly for the fly, then zip back to its lie. On the second cast, it tilts up and tracks the fly for a few more inches before gliding back down to the bottom. On the third cast, I twitch the fly, and that usually does it. The fish takes solidly. Then again, plenty of other times a trout will wallop the fly the moment it touches down, as if it had been waiting its whole life for my Stimulator to drift past. And then there are the fingerlings barely larger than the fly itself that zip up and down five or six times without ever taking. I admire their moxie.

But even with all this casting, accuracy is key. Cast two inches off the mark, and you might as well have sliced it into the willow branch dangling two feet above the pool. But if I miss, I simply make another cast and another and another until I get it right. My scorecard is not in swings. If that was the case, my handicap would be in the hundreds.

Nearly all of this runs heretical to most of what I've read about fishing small trout streams, which talk about crawling around on hands and knees and getting in one good cast before the entire pool spooks. On this particular rushing mountain brook, it just doesn't happen that way, and I'm glad.

Speaking of keeping score, I tend not to count trout actually landed but instead how many individual fish I can get to take a pass at the fly. Because I use larger imitations, many of the smaller fish simply can't eat them, which is not a bad thing, as I don't necessarily want to impale a three-inch trout on a size eight hook. If one fish comes up but never commits, either because it was too small or too scrutinizing, it counts. And why shouldn't it? It was a wild trout, willing to rise to a dry fly, by God.

I have learned that the best time to fish—at least my favorite time—is after a summer thunderstorm. Preferably one that rolled in the night before, dropped a half-inch of rain, and left the stream high but clearing the next morning. That's when trout seem to materialize out of nowhere, and nearly every promising-looking spot produces at least a rise or two. The very best way to fish during those magical times is in wading sandals, shorts, and a T-shirt.

Entering the stream at the bottom of the property and working my way upstream, feeling the bracing chill of cold water on my feet, and then the even colder pockets where springs seep in, making short casts on the two-weight and raising trout after trout on dry flies, is about as intimate a kind of angling as I can imagine. During these poststorm sessions, I have raised more than 30 trout in less than an hour.

As far as I can tell, I am the only angler who consistently fishes the stream. Virtually its entire length is posted except at the very mouth, which used to have a rusted sign that proclaimed a short stretch a "public fishing stream." But because there was virtually no parking, I'm not sure how you were supposed to access it. But even if you could fish it, I don't see anglers flocking here, particularly when the nearby Delaware contains trout that run several orders of magnitude larger.

Still, we did catch a poacher on the stream once, or rather Mimi did. It happened on an Indian summer day in October after trout season had closed. I was at the hardware store in town, so I missed the whole thing, but when I returned Mimi was still laughing about it. She said she walked out on the porch and saw a 12-year-old boy on the other side of the stream, bait fishing in the pool directly in front of the cabin. His bicycle was propped up against a tree. She thought she recognized him as one of the grandkids of the farmer down the road. She walked out to talk to him—not necessarily to kick him off—but just to let him know the season was closed. When he saw her, she said he immediately looked scared, like he got caught doing something he wasn't supposed to be doing.

"How's the fishing?" she asked.

"Ummm, OK, I guess," he said sheepishly.

Then she said as nicely as she could, "You know, I'm not positive, but I'm pretty sure trout season is closed."

He shifted uncomfortably and said, "Oh. Well. I'm not keeping any anyway."

Then he reached into his pocket, pulled out a still-wriggling six-inch brook trout, and threw it back into the stream. Then he got on his bike and rode away, never to return.

By the end of the first year of fishing the stream, I had catalogued my favorite pools. The aforementioned Shipwreck was certainly a favorite, and I chronicled the first wild rainbow I took there with this simple entry in my fishing journal: "Caught a seven-inch rainbow in the Shipwreck Pool that jumped three times—a plump, perfect trout." Below the Shipwreck, closer to the cabin, a flat narrowed and pinched the current hard against the far bank, where three yellow birches clung. Over time, the stream had scalloped a ten-foot long, knee-deep run that partially undercut the roots of the birches and provided perfect overhead cover for trout. I could sit by the fire pit, sip a beer, and watch brookies rise to midges at the tail-out. This became almost as fun as actually casting for them. Between there and the Shipwreck, there was a lovely spot where the stream flowed over a smooth, tabletop-sized river rock, then dropped a foot into a thigh-deep plunge pool that always held a choice fish or two. I remember peering into it once and seeing a dead eight-inch brook trout being scavenged by a crayfish. Old age, I guess. And then there was the dogleg two-thirds of the way up my property, where a logjam slowed the current, the stream deepened, and trout frequently rose. Again, my journal reveals I caught a nine-inch "monster male brookie" there.

There were other spots, too: the felled hemlock deliberately placed across the stream—presumably by the old owner. It dammed the flow and created a nice run above and deep hole below. And the waist-deep pool below the culvert, while technically not on my property, was always an excellent place to sometimes see up to a dozen terrified trout darting about as soon as I peeked into it from the road up above.

Yes, those were my favorite pools on the stream. They were guarded by mature shade trees; the woods adjacent to them were ferny and dark. I knew them intimately for a few glorious seasons, and I caught wild trout virtually whenever I cast a dry fly onto their rushing, clear waters.

But they are all gone now. Obliterated.

May 7: Great Hendrickson and caddis hatches this weekend, with plenty of fish looking up. I fished Saturday in the Delaware for about 90 minutes and hooked four, including a brute that actually broke my hook (first trout that ever did that to me). I managed to land two browns—including a hook-jawed male of 18 inches and a football 13-incher—and jumped another that looked about 16 inches.

But the highlight took place on Sunday on the stream, which was running high and clear. Last September's miniflood carved a very trouty hole directly in front of the cabin. It's one of the few places on the stream that has a genuine undercut bank shored up by the roots of a few birch trees.

I drop a small Stimulator at the head of the pool with my two-weight, hoping for a six-inch brookie. I watch the fly and notice what at first looks like a river rock mysteriously moving underneath it. Then the rock materializes into a rainbow trout—a big one—16 inches. The fish tracks the fly for a few feet, then changes its mind and casually glides back to the undercut.

I actually get goose bumps, as this fish is clearly a spawner that had run up the stream, jumped a culvert and a few three-foot waterfalls, and has now found refuge in the undercut bank. And it is hungry. There had been decent Hendrickson hatches on the creek, so it probably decided to stay and feed before low water will force it to drop back to the big river.

I make another cast—there it is again, moving for the fly but coming up short at the last second. This requires a change in tactics. I retie my leader, lengthen the tippet, put on boots and my vest. I am no longer screwing around. I make sure I have my camera in my vest—a jinx, but I don't care. Then I wade across the stream and approach the pool from a better angle downstream.

I crouch and drop the fly into the sweet spot. The trout comes up and it takes it cleanly. I lift and it is on—and then it's off. Nooo! I decide to rest it for as long as I can bear it. I back off and wade out of the stream and have a quick lunch. Then I try again . . . but nothing . . . and again with the same result.

Then Finn decides he wants in on the action. He reminds me he is a fly fisherman—a six-year-old fly fisherman—so I hand him the rod before wisely clipping off the fly. He flogs the water and air around him to a maelstrom, culminating his performance by whacking me in the face with the rod.

Soon it was time to drive home to New Jersey. No rain this week, so I'm expecting the fish will drop back to the big river—the only large trout I've seen along my stretch since owning the place.

Floods, Damn Floods, and Time to Call Noah

I stupidly thought the first flood at the cabin was kind of fun. There are pictures of me grinning dumbly next to the washed-out road above the culvert. They were taken the morning after Tropical Storm Ivan clipped the Catskills in September 2004. It hit on a Friday night, and I had driven straight from work through increasingly heavy rains until I pulled into the driveway at around eight o'clock. I unlocked the back door, turned on the lights, and cracked the jalousie windows on the porch. Then I opened a bottle of beer and sat—all snug and warm—listening to the rain pour down and the stream rush past. "Let it rain!" I thought.

Idiot.

After a while, I could distinguish that one of the sounds was slowly overtaking the other—the stream. It was morphing from a tinny hiss to a deep, voluminous roar. I grabbed a flashlight, opened the porch door, and shined it through the rain down to the water. Yes, it certainly looked high and muddy but no more so than after a strong thunderstorm. I went back inside and continued enjoying my beer.

Then Mimi showed up—also right from work. She described a harrowing drive through rain so heavy she could hardly see the road. She went into the bedroom to dry off and change, and then joined me on the cozy porch. Meanwhile the sound of the

stream continued to grow louder, and I found myself periodically checking the water level with the flashlight. At first it was lapping against the base of a rock wall maybe 15 feet away. Then it had climbed past the second row of rocks. Then the third.

At that point I may have wished for the first time that the rain would stop.

But it didn't, and with the stream now roaring wildly, we had to talk over it to be heard. I checked the water level again, and by now it had inched up to the top of the wall no more than six vertical feet from the cabin. I knew the streambank on the other side was technically lower, so if the water did spill over the bank, it should technically do so over there. But with the decibel levels now approaching Niagara Falls, this didn't necessarily comfort me.

Then we heard the first conga drum.

It was a single, low, percussive "thunk" coming from somewhere upstream. Mimi and I looked at each other. There it was again, except closer—and then closer still. Then it was right in front of the cabin and then downstream. We realized the sound came from a dislodged boulder bouncing along the stream bottom. Another one came from upstream. And another. Then, slowly an entire African percussion section began. Admittedly, we found these strange noises amusing. We would chuckle at the mix of high-pitched smaller rocks and the deep bass of larger ones ping-ponging their way downstream.

Eventually the rain began to slow, and it looked like the stream had finally stopped rising, so we went to bed. We closed the porch door behind us to drown out the sound of raging water. But I slept fitfully, waking up every hour or so to venture onto the porch. Each time I would open the door, I'd step onto what sounded like a subway platform, complete with a quartet of street musicians continuing to thump away on their drums.

Morning came, and the rain had stopped. The stream was still a brown torrent, though it had dropped at least a foot from the night before. I walked outside, and at first, it looked like it had largely behaved and stayed within its banks. Then I looked downstream and saw that I was mistaken. The rocks and boulders we had heard migrating the night before had all settled in front of the culvert, which had become blocked by a logjam of branches, root balls, and other flotsam. Now, a 20-foot-long shoal of cobble rose from the stream like some newly minted volcanic island.

The road above the culvert had not fared well. With the pipe clogged, sometime overnight the water rose until it breached. Then, like an uncaged animal, it raked and tore at the roadbed, carving deep troughs into it. Mimi and I put on rubber boots and waded across what was left. Then we continued down the road to discover that two other crossings had suffered similar fates. But besides these washouts, overall, the six-foot-wide stream seemed just fine.

Not so on the Delaware. We drove to check on a friend's weekend cabin on the Pennsylvania side of the river. Normally his home is set back 100 yards from the riverbank and stands on a wooded plateau a good 15 feet above the water. When I turned into his driveway, I saw instead what looked like the floating house on the Amazon in the *várzea*. My friend and his wife stood on their front porch waving. Brown river water lapped all around their front steps. I immediately put on waders and attempted to continue down their submerged driveway, but the water quickly deepened. My friend called over the low rumble of the flooded river, assuring me he was OK. He said the water already started to drop, and he had a canoe tied to the other side of the house and would paddle to the shoreline in the afternoon. Later he would tell me how he, his wife, and his dog almost swamped trying to navigate around flooded trees in deceptively strong currents.

But there, too, eventually the waters receded. By the next week, the road in front of the cabin was repaired and the culvert cleared of rocks and debris by the town. Meteorological experts would later call it a 100-year flood, meaning that, on average, such an event would happen just once a century. Key words here: "on average."

I never really saw the next flood, which took place in April 2005, firsthand, though I do know experts consider it worse than Ivan and have dubbed it a 500-year "storm event." Our son, Finn, was born in early February, and we hadn't opened the cabin yet when it struck. A few days before it hit, on April 1—opening day of trout season—I fished with a friend on the Neversink, a large Delaware tributary. In many ways, it was a classic opener with high, cold water and a dearth of cooperative trout. We drove from spot to spot anyway, trying in vain to find at least a hatching stonefly or something to give us hope. Eventually, we came to a settlement of old cabins on the lower river a few miles from where it meets the Delaware. I remember thinking that many of the houses, some of which appeared to be converted into year-round residences, looked to be built right on the flood plain. Three days later, virtually all of them would be underwater.

A muscular low-pressure system would settle over the Catskills, unleashing another several inches of rain on an already-saturated watershed. The Neversink, Delaware, and other rivers in the area surged up to 10 vertical feet over their banks. Hundreds of houses suffered major damage, with dozens destroyed outright or later condemned. My friend in Pennsylvania reported that his house had six feet of water in his basement. Later he would find schools of dried minnows in his garage. He told me how he watched—terrified—as the river came just inches from spilling into his living room before it finally receded.

But when we opened our cabin later in the month, all seemed well. We could see a rack line of debris where the stream had come up, and we heard from our neighbors that the road had once again washed out at each of the stream crossings. But it had since been repaired, and when I walked the stream, most of the pools looked the same. Just the upstream dogleg had filled in with a few inches of river rock. Overall, we felt lucky and quickly forgot about floods and other unpleasantries.

Fast forward to late June 2006. The forecast sounded harmless enough: chance of thunderstorms later on Sunday and continuing into the night. Rain heavy at times. But this was early summer, not the time of tropical storms or nasty nor'easters. Let it rain.

We had company that weekend: my friend Jim; his wife, Kathy; and their two boys. We spent a lazy Saturday around the cabin. Jim's boys explored the woods and the stream. Our son Finn, now a year and a half, watched and napped. Later we enjoyed a peaceful campfire that went late into the night after the kids all fell asleep. The next morning, under increasingly cloudy skies, Jim decided to show off his engineering skills by demonstrating how to construct cairns from river rocks. After much balancing and a few harmless collapses, he built a beauty: a sturdy multilayered seven-footer just a few feet from the stream. Its base was shored up with larger boulders that he had rolled from the far bank. Each subsequent layer was made up of a flat rock carefully stabilized with perfectly fitted round stones for balance. It was an engineering masterpiece.

Then someone said, "Now *that* tower will last a long time."

Just then it started to lightly rain.

We had lunch as the rain grew steadier. Then we decided to call it a weekend. By the time Jim and his family left and we had closed up the cabin, I noticed the stream had come up a few inches and was starting to run slightly off-color. Typical summer storm. We headed home, and I didn't give the stream another thought.

For the first hour during our ride home, it continued to pour. But then the skies began to clear, and by the time we crossed into New Jersey, the sun was shining. Little did we know that, back at the cabin, the apocalypse had begun.

The next day, I started to hear news reports of extensive flooding in the Catskills. The low-pressure system that brought the thunderstorms had stalled, and freakish amounts of rain fell over the region. The *New York Times* ran a front-page story showing a Sunoco gas station on the nearby Beaverkill with just the top of the sign visible under what looked like the Mississippi. I immediately began calling my neighbors up the road, but the phones weren't working. Not good. I called my friend in Pennsylvania. It turned out he didn't come up for the weekend. He could only relay a brief message he received from one of his contacts on the river: Record flooding. Disaster area. Don't try to come up.

The news worsened. A 15-year-old girl drowned in the town of Livingston Manor when the Willowemoc Creek jumped its banks. Near Binghamton, a highway buckled from flash flooding, and two truckers were killed when they drove into the chasm. I kept calling my neighbors but still couldn't get through.

Then, on Friday, someone answered. It was Tim's mom, Marian. She quickly said everyone was OK. They had company visiting from out of state when the storm hit. The kids thought it was exciting to be marooned for several days. Now power had just come back on. There were FEMA trucks all over the place. Lots of roads still washed out.

Then I asked, "Marian, is my cabin OK?"

She said, "Yes, we took a look, and it's fine."

But I could tell there was more to it.

"How about the property, the stream?" I asked.

She said soberly, "Steve, you're not going to like it."

Rather than ask what she meant, all I said was "OK. See you tomorrow." And I hung up.

I drove up alone early the next day. Mimi stayed home with Finn, agreeing that a federal disaster area was no place for a toddler. I couldn't think of what to possibly bring with me, so all I packed was my camera, a few bottles of water, and some lunch. Looking back, a hip flask filled with something really strong might have been a good idea, too.

Not surprisingly, driving there proved difficult. Most of the secondary roads I normally took were still closed, so I had to stick to highways. As I dropped into the Beaverkill Valley, I started to see gullies, laid open and raw, cut into many of the hillsides from flash flooding. The Beaverkill itself still ran high and muddy but was no longer at flood stage. Same with the East Branch of the Delaware, though many downed trees could be seen lining the riverbanks.

When I finally made the turn down the long road that led to the cabin, my palms were sweaty, and my heart pounded. It was a hot, summery day, and the road was thick with dust that turned out to be dried mud from various washouts. I passed Tim's house, then Marian's. All looked fine except for some smaller gullies running alongside the road. Then I pulled into the driveway. At first I thought, "Marian was right: The cabin looks absolutely fine. It stood there almost defiantly as if saying, 'What flood?'" The usual complement of early summer birds—vireos, redstarts, indigo buntings—called as they did before we drove home a week earlier. But then beyond the house itself, where the stream ran, there was something new, something alien: sunlight. I slowly walked around the back for a better look.

The world had changed.

I stopped and stood with my hands on my hips and stared for a long time. It took me a while to comprehend exactly what I was seeing. I remember thinking it looked like a sort of split screen: On one side, the cabin as it always had been with, the green, verdant hillside continuing upward behind it. And on the other side? A lifeless, barren, desecrated moonscape.

Where to begin? First of all, the entire course of the stream had moved—*moved*—yards closer to the cabin. It now loomed a few feet from the shed, threatening to undermine and topple it. The stream had torn through the yard, nearly taking out the bunkhouse. A logjam of debris had collected under one of its supports. The top layer of rocks from the firepit—some weighing 20 or 30 pounds—had simply washed away. The streambanks, instead of sloping gently and pleasantly, were now cut vertically like a scale-model Grand Canyon. One wrong step, and down you'd go four feet or more. The stream itself—now ironically running low because it hadn't rained in almost a week—looked milky and sickly. Rocks on the bottom appeared raw and newly unearthed.

And then there was the elephant in the room—or, more accurately, a herd of them. On the far bank—just a few feet from where I stood—and extending far upriver was my own personal rock quarry. And not a small one. Thousands of cubic yards of river rock, gravel, and sand—some of it five feet deep—had smothered most of the dark, shady, ferny, magical woods. And speaking of woods—what woods? A hundred trees had vanished like they were beamed up by aliens. Entire groves of mature hemlocks, spruce, ash, birch, and maple that lined the stream a week ago were simply no longer there, replaced instead by nothing but sun-blasted cobble.

Then I looked downstream and could see where many of the trees had wound up. A logjam bigger than my cabin lodged against what was left of the culvert. I looked back at the stream. The shade trees were gone, the trout pools were gone, presumably the trout were gone, and the bugs were gone. Gone, gone, gone.

I stood silently for another minute. A wood peewee called cheerfully, "*Pee-weeeee!*" Shut the hell up.

I wandered down the driveway to the road for another perspective. Below the culvert, much of the dirt road had washed away along with many more mature trees that once lined it. In some places there were ten-foot-deep craters where the stream decided to body-slam the roadbed—probably after a few wayward trees and their respective root balls temporarily clogged the channel. You could see striations of rock and rubble like some great archaeological dig had taken place.

Just then a Humvee with a FEMA logo came slowly bouncing along the road. It pulled up next to me in a small cloud of dust, and down rolled a tinted window. A man in his early 30s with close-cropped hair and sunglasses looked at me. I could feel the cold blast of air conditioning from inside the Hummer.

"Everything OK?" he asked.

I wasn't sure what to say. Some people lost their entire homes, others their lives. My friend in Pennsylvania had five feet of fetid, muddy river water in his living room. I lost a trout stream. But still, coffee and some donuts from the Red Cross were not going to fix this problem.

"Yep. I'm fine," was all I said.

I took a few pictures of the damage, stopped briefly to talk to Marian and Tim, and headed home. I believe I skipped lunch.

So what the hell happened? I talked to a friend of mine who does stream restoration work for the Environmental Protection Agency. He did some research and told me that the drainage received an astounding 15 inches of rain in a two-day period—a 700-year storm event. Not that one needs additional perspective, but if that much rain fell as snow, it would have completely buried the entire cabin so just the very top of the chimney showed. With all that water essentially trapped in a narrow watershed, it turned into a colossal firehose—the kind strip-miners use to take out the sides of mountains. How much water ran into the stream? My friend crunched some additional numbers: He estimated that, based on gauges in nearby rivers like the East Branch of the Delaware, the six-foot-wide stream, which on average runs at a little less than five cubic feet of water per second, had skyrocketed to 68 times its normal flow, or 340 cubic feet per second. That is the average summertime flow of the Beaverkill, a 100-foot-wide trout river. Cram 100 feet of river into a six-foot-wide brook, and bad things will happen.

Tim believes a flash flood brought down a wall of water and debris that caused much of the damage. Entire hillsides upstream were certainly wiped clean of trees. If they washed into the stream all at once, they could have lodged in some obstruction and formed a dam. Pressure would have built, and finally the whole thing would smash open like King Kong busting down the wall on Skull Island. Tim talked to a farmer who said he saw full-grown hemlocks pinwheeling downriver, the current pushing them end over end like in a giant water wheel.

My friend at the EPA was more scientific, writing,

The anomalously high flood flow overtopped and eroded stream banks, transported trees and other woody debris downstream, and greatly increased stream bedload. Boulders greater than 12 inches in diameter were readily transported downstream during this event. Large hemlock, birch and other trees lining the stream were toppled, removed, and deposited as debris dams in many locations. In lower-gradient reaches of the stream, large sediment deposits occurred. In the lower reach, significant sediment deposition occurred, causing a channel avulsion.

Whether it was anomalously high flood flow, channel avulsion, or King Kong, one thing is for damn sure: The stream and the adjoining woodland never had a chance.

I drove back the following Saturday. When I first stood gawking at the destruction the week before, I noticed that the rock wall directly in front of the cabin—the one I had used as a measuring gauge during Ivan, had partially collapsed into the stream. It looked like the wall may have actually helped save the bank from eroding by shunting away some of the current before it finally toppled—heroically, I like to think. In any case, I was determined to fix it. Given how utterly trashed the rest of the landscape was— the massive amount of downed trees, the small glacier of river rocks literally now in my backyard—I obviously was not thinking clearly. But still I needed to do something—anything—to begin bringing the stream back and restoring the landscape. So I drove up again with lunch, water, and a pair of work gloves.

But when I arrived and once more took in the scope of the destruction before me, I began to realize what a fool's errand I had set out on. I stepped into the stream and stood in front of the collapsed wall wearing my silly gloves. I looked upstream at no fewer than literally a million new river rocks. Then I looked downstream at a mountain of lumber straight out of one of those historical photos on the great logging rafts from the 1800s. Fixing a few feet of rock wall felt as futile as grabbing a broom and sweeping up a little after the fire-bombing of Dresden.

Thankfully, that's when I saw the man standing on the road. He waved, and I waved back. Then he called out something, but I couldn't hear him. I decided this was the perfect excuse to abandon the rock wall project, so I got out of the stream to see what he wanted. It turned out he was the foreman of the contractor FEMA hired to fix the flood-damaged road. He wanted to see how I was doing. I told him about the stream and how the channel had moved and was now a few feet from taking out my shed and also threatening my bunkhouse.

Then he told me about the emergency permits being issued by the New York State Department of Environmental Conservation. He said the state gave a temporary blanket permit for all landowners who needed to protect their structures from further damage. You needn't apply for it; just go ahead and do whatever it takes.

He pointed to the stream in front of the cabin and said, "My crew can fix this."

Just then, I heard the low rumble of an enormous piece of earth-moving equipment working a few hundred yards downstream. I looked and saw a front-end loader move a 500-pound rock from the road as if it were brushing away dandruff.

"That's one of my guys," he said.

And so it came to pass that I hired his crew to literally move the stream back to its original channel—preflood, at least—and to remove the Grand Canyon effect by grading the stream banks back to a more gradual, gentle slope. Along with this, the cabin-sized logjam and other fallen trees would be moved off site. Lastly, he would throw down some dirt to give something—anything—a chance to grow on top of the new rock quarry.

This was not an easy decision for me. The idea of running heavy equipment in the stream was anathema. I had seen firsthand the effects of channelization on small marginal creeks back home in New Jersey for various "flood control" projects. The end result was often a near-lifeless waterway overrun with poison ivy and invasive species like Japanese knotweed. Now I was paying someone to do this very thing to a wild, native trout stream—*my* wild, native trout stream.

We had a long talk about the job, and I asked him to please save as many of the standing trees as possible. He said he would do the best he could. It felt like I was pleading to a surgeon in the pre-op room about how I still wanted a good quality of life when I woke up from the anesthesia.

A few weeks later, the foreman called me to let me know that the work was done. Mimi and I drove up, and yes, they had done as good a job as could be expected. They pushed the stream channel back to where it ran before the flood. It looked fine—in a sterile, Los Angeles River sort of way. It was precisely the width of a bulldozer blade and three inches deep—no rifles or pools. The banks were graded as promised. Some trees remained; others had to be removed to get the equipment where it needed to go.

The foreman, whom I believe was a genuinely nice person, knew I was a fisherman and had his crew place a few boulders here and there midstream. When I paid him, he assured me the fish would come back.

"Just give it time," he said.

I nodded, and I looked at the gray, lifeless streambanks and the still-milky water. I thought of the forever-lost pools where trout once rose freely in the dark shade of the woodland. The words from the letter written to me by the previous owner's son echoed:

A little cabin in the woods with a picturesque stream, native trout, great hemlocks, magical tree roots, ferns, and rocks. A fairy land for young children and young at heart.

That's when I made a pledge that I would do whatever it takes to restore the six-foot-wide trout stream.

May 13: The whole thing sounds screwy. I'm standing thigh-deep in the East Branch of the Delaware, more than 300 river miles from the head of the tide, casting a fly for a saltwater fish that's not even technically eating. And when it's done spawning a few weeks from now and starts to feed again, it will daintily sip mayflies and caddis. But right now, on this morning in mid-May, all it wants to do is chase down bright chartreuse streamers stripped fast, like a fleeing baitfish—even though it's not known as a fish eater. Like I said, it's screwy.

But that's how American shad roll, and I do my best to roll with them.

I've waded out to a shoal of cobble just far enough into the river so I won't snag any streamside brush behind me on a back cast. In front of me, I can see larger submerged boulders give way to the darker, deeper water of the river channel. Hopefully shad are holding somewhere off the bottom.

My gear is strange, too. I'm using a burly nine-foot seven-weight fly rod with a fast-sinking shooting line. My leader is beyond basic—two feet of straight ten-pound-test monofilament. My fly is just some chartreuse ice chenille wound around a size 8 saltwater hook with some calf-tail hairs tied in at the end—an add-on that I'm sure is totally unnecessary but makes me feel good. Last, I use the quintessential saltwater fly-rodder's gear: a stripping basket buckled to my waist to gather loose line. On this trout river, I look as misplaced as a tweedy dry fly angler standing in the surf at Montauk waiting for a mayfly hatch.

I strip arm-lengths of line from the reel into the basket. Then I roll-cast the shooting head, pick it up with the rod, and double-haul it as far as I can. But my timing is slightly off, and it lands in a heap 30 feet away. So I strip it partway back and roll the head out again. Before the fly touches down, I haul back once, then forward, and shoot.

Yards of coiled running line zip up the guides and out into the river. The fly lands 70 feet away. Better.

I let the line sink for a few seconds and then begin stripping it back—fast, like I was fishing for bluefish or barracuda on the high seas. Again, weird. But I was taught by the master: an angler named Rich Fasanello, who in turn was taught by Catskill legend Harry Darbee in the 1960s. Rich strips as fast as he can pull the line and hooks shad with almost mechanical efficiency. I once saw him outfish a half-dozen shad fishermen, all of whom threw darts on spinning gear. The score was 25 to 0. The other anglers had clustered around Rich, frantically casting as he hooked shad after shad on his fly rod. I thought Rich might get thrown in.

My line tightens, and I raise the rod to set the hook. Wrong. I just pulled the fly from the fish's mouth. Instead I should have strip-set, another saltwater move where you pull down hard with your stripping hand to set the hook but keep the rod pointed toward the fish. Lift the rod, as I just did, and you'll swing and miss nearly every time. I need to remind myself I am not trout fishing—hard to do when caddis are bouncing off the river and I hear a Canada warbler and a hermit thrush trading calls in the woods behind me.

A few casts later, the line tightens again. I strip hard once, then twice, until I feel the full weight of the shad through the line and into my hand. It's solidly hooked, so I raise the rod and reel up slack line as fast I can. Just as the fish is on the reel, it takes off on a run that ends in a clean leap. It runs some more and then cartwheels, sending up a halo of spray.

The fish now planes away from me, and the rod bends deeply, absorbing pressure. I'm once more amazed that this shad has swum literally 300 miles against the current and is now beating up my gear—all on an empty stomach. It zips off on another shorter run, then changes direction, and swims toward me. I see it now a few yards away in clear river water. In the morning sun, it glows blueish-silver. A nice roe—close to five pounds. Three smaller male shad follow it, wondering *if its sudden acrobatics means it's ready to spawn. Take it easy, fellas; maybe later.*

I bring the shad closer until I can grab the fly line, then I slide the fish so I can brace it against the downstream leg of my waders. Shad have no handles—you can't lip them like a bass or tail them. They writhe back and forth constantly as you try to unhook them, and I can feel the power and drive that sent this one through rapids and unrelenting current to finally hole up here in a trout pool.

I slide the fly from the fish's scooped mouth and look at its belly bulging with roe. Earlier in the season, this fish would have been dinner. I'd have bled it on the spot, then taken it home and baked it and cooked its roe using author John McPhee's foolproof and delicious method of steaming it on a thick bed of bacon. Many anglers scoff at the eating qualities of shad, complaining about bones and likening them to menhaden—a notoriously oily baitfish. All I can say is this: more for me.

But with the fish this far upriver and some of its delicious fat reserves burned up, I opt to let it go. It kicks its tail, then glides back to the river channel, and vanishes. Later this evening, when I'm casting dry flies for rising trout, I may see it torpedoing across the river chased by males in their spawning dance.

Then later in June, the shad may fool me by rising like a trout at dusk, scooping mayflies from the surface. I may hook it by accident. But by then it will be a mere shadow—all head without much fight left. I will sheepishly release it again. If it's lucky, it will fill its fuel tank with enough bugs to make it downriver and to the sea—dodging eagles and osprey, then eventually sharks and tuna. It will reach its feeding grounds in the Bay of Fundy, where it will gorge on plankton and krill. Next spring it will run the river and maybe even wind up in this same trout pool, larger and stronger and ready to beat up my strange tackle some more.

Build It, and They Will Rise

"Thalweg." "Vortex Rocks." "Revetments." The words in the book sounded like medieval weaponry and battle tactics. Instead I was poring through a manual called *Restoring Streams in Cities* by Ann L. Riley. Because the six-foot-wide stream now resembled an urbanized river, it seemed like an appropriate place to start.

I found myself neck-deep in new terminology. Thalweg was simply the lowest point along any horizontal line across a streambed; vortex rocks were placed to create either pools or riffles, using the power of moving water to do most of the excavating; and revetments were batteries of stone or brush to prevent a bank from further eroding.

The book showed proud armies of volunteers cleaning garbage from urban waterways and using heavy machinery to resculpt degraded creek channels. But because I was an army of one or maybe two at best and the heaviest machinery I had was a shovel, I decided to focus on the section about "soil bioengineering"—the use of live plants to restore streambanks.

It contained tantalizing "before" and "after" images of a restored stream. The "before" image looked sadly familiar: a denuded creek with a sterile-looking drainage ditch oozing through it. The "after" image was unrecognizable: growth so lush you could hardly see the water anymore—all just a year after installing something called "live willow stakes." What, in God's name, were these magic

stakes? I learned that many species of willows have the ability to reroot if you simply take a cutting from a live tree and insert it into the soil. This can be done using a branch as little as an inch in diameter. The best time is in the fall, when the trees go dormant. By the next spring, the stakes begin to root and bud. Willow roots are particularly fibrous and can armor a bank from erosion—at least according to the book. This seemed like the perfect entry-level restoration project for me to attempt.

Luckily, I had a nearby source for willows: a swampy five-acre thicket next to Tim's house. Up to that point, I had known it only as a birding hot spot, particularly for yellowthroats, redstarts, song sparrows, and a relatively rare alder flycatcher that showed up one spring. Now, hopefully, it would become a wellspring for new growth along the stream. I asked Tim if I could cut down a few small trees, explaining what I planned to use them for. He said with his usual generosity, "Take as many as you want."

So on a Saturday in October, I sawed down four willows, each maybe 15 feet tall. Then I cut each tree into a dozen live stakes ranging from a foot to 14 inches long. I made sure to angle the bottom part of the stake, both for ease of installation and as a reminder not to plant them upside down. Willows don't know which way is up, according to the book. Plant them the wrong way and their branches grow into the ground. After I cut and trimmed them, I soaked the stakes overnight in a bucket of water, which apparently helps with later root growth and budding.

The book showed images of muddy-looking stream banks where you could simply shove in each stake by hand or tap it in with a rubber mallet. I was not so lucky. The pervasiveness of rocks and more rocks, coupled with the fact that any mud or silt seemed to have been blown into the Atlantic by the flood, made finding a soft spot to push in a stake extremely difficult.

Instead I wound up using a five-pound sledgehammer and a length of two-inch steel pipe to drive in a pilot hole. When the pipe eventually bent and broke, I switched to a heavy-duty iron land-surveyor's stake called a frost pin.

It felt like hard labor—in a prison-sentence sort of way. All I needed was a striped uniform and leg irons. I banged away at the frost pin with the sledgehammer. Sometimes I'd smash my way through river rocks and force in a pilot hole. Other times I'd thud into some unseen slab of bedrock, making my hands sting like I hit a 95-mile-an-hour fastball in the middle of November. I cursed and sweated, longing for my two-weight, which was quickly gathering dust on the nearby porch. Ibuprofen and a beer at the end of the day made things slightly better.

Over the course of a long weekend, I managed to stake 50 willows into a 75-foot stretch of streambank. As per the book's instructions, I installed them as close as I could to the waterline (sometimes near the thalweg, of course). Apparently, willows "like their feet wet," and I obliged them. I chose the stretch closest to the culvert simply because it was hit with the greatest damage from the flood and subsequent channelization. Plus, I could stare at my handiwork from the front porch. When I was done, it didn't look like much, just a bunch of sticks poking up here and there from an otherwise bare streambank. The following weekend, we closed the cabin for the season.

Over the winter, my friend Paul, a forester with the state of Rhode Island, had mentioned that many states offer a seedling program, where landowners can purchase one- to two-year-old bare-root trees in bulk at a deeply discounted rate. The state sees this as a good investment: More trees planted mean better wildlife habitat or less erosion or, down the road, more timber sales (and presumably tax revenue). I learned that New York State did in fact offer such a program, and on January 2, the first day you could place an order, I went nuts.

First, I ordered 100 spruce trees to replace many of those washed away during the flood, then I ordered 100 white pines, then two 100-count riparian packets—an assortment of water-loving and streambank-stabilizing trees and shrubs. Then for good measure, I threw in 100 sandbar willows, an erosion-resistant species known to grow quickly and provide shade.

All told, 500 trees were coming, each of which would have to be individually planted in rock—I mean soil. No, I mean rock. Let's call it rocky soil. Or how about soil-y rock. In any case, come spring, they would all need to go into the ground. I called Jim and reserved him for the last weekend in April, tempting him with the possibility of a Hendrickson hatch on the Delaware. I dubbed it a "plant and cast" weekend.

That February, Mimi and I checked on the cabin as we do at least once or twice each winter, just to make sure a tree hasn't fallen on it or a grouse hasn't flown into a storm window (yes, that happened once). When we were done making sure all was well inside, I wandered down to the stream to check on the willow stakes. There was little snow on the ground that winter, and the water was up a few inches from a recent rain. Many of the stakes were either partially submerged or sticking up just along the edge of the waterline. All of them still looked like sticks, nothing more. On the whole, the stream, bare, gray, and seemingly lifeless, looked particularly bleak.

When spring came, we were not in a rush to open the cabin, so we held off until mid-April. Then one Saturday, we packed the car, and we packed up Finn, now two years old, and headed north. When we got there, the stream thankfully looked a little better. Though some of the banks had eroded from some late-winter storms, the Los Angeles River look was beginning to wane, replaced by the beginnings of a typical trout stream's riffle-pool sequence. Even the tops of some of the buried boulders now showed here and there.

After we unpacked, I walked down to my restoration project to lament my 50 sticks, I mean stakes. And there they were, still just sitting there looking the same as they had since I literally smashed rocks to drive them in the ground six months earlier.

I squatted down next to one trying to figure out what I did wrong. Maybe it was the lack of soil, or maybe I planted them too late or too early. But then I spotted something on the bark—some sort of reddish nodes sticking out here and there. I touched one and it was tender. *Buds.* I quickly checked the other stakes. Virtually all of them were swollen with buds, too.

I ran back to the cabin to tell Mimi, who was mid-diaper-change with Finn. "We've got buds on the willows!" I yelled. I leaned over to tell Finn, "Buds on the willows, Finn! Trees are coming back. Maybe the trout will come back!"

Finn seemed happy, but it was probably the fresh diaper.

Two weeks later, the seedlings arrived upstate, and I was ready for them. I had just ordered through a catalog an "extreme planting bar"—ten pounds of forged steel designed to dig holes in the rockiest soil. It looked like something Vikings would have used in warfare (a thalweg?).

Jim met me at my house early on a warm Saturday morning, armed with a pry bar that looked like it could topple a full-grown oak. Mimi and Finn wished us well but smartly remained at home. A two-year-old, 500 trees, and cranky men donning heavy steel tools did not seem like a good combination.

About a half-hour from the cabin, I began to hear the light patter of rain hitting the windshield. Strange, because it was sunny. Then I realized it was the splatter of many tiny insects. Blackflies. This was not going to be a pleasant day of gardening.

The seedlings had to be picked up at the office of a local forester. I signed for the order and put bag after bag in the back of my car. The forester looked at the order, then Jim and me, and said, "You guys are going to be busy." Just then, the first blackfly bit me behind the ear.

The next several hours might best be imagined as a movie montage. "Song of the Volga Boatmen" plays. There is sweat and toil. Hundreds and hundreds of seedlings are unbagged and placed in buckets of water. When I first open the bags, I am surprised how small some of them are—barely six inches tall; others are longer but resemble leafless buggy whips. I imagine the years it will take for these to grow in, and it strikes me that soil bioengineering is not for the impatient. Then planting bars are wielded mightily. They ricochet off rocks, sometimes literally sending up sparks. But occasionally they strike pay dirt in the form of a rare-as-gold pocket of good soil. Meanwhile, entire dance troupes of blackflies have entered the scene, pirouetting around our heads. Jim repeatedly plays the old camper's trick of standing next to me, then pretending to tie his shoe and backing away hunched over, thus transferring his blackfly squadron to my own sweaty noggin.

The spruces went in first. We planted a few dozen along the road to begin to reestablish the thick wall of green that gave the cabin so much privacy before the flood. Others went in close to the stream but set back a few feet in case the newly formed banks eroded any further. Then came the pines, and again we stuck some in along the road and the rest along the stream. Each riparian packet contained bundles of different wetland-loving species marked with a label. There were five species of shrub: red osier dogwood, buttonbush, swamp rose, arrowwood, and cranberry viburnum; and five trees: sycamore, red oak, white spruce, pussy willow, and something called a hybrid poplar. We planted these next and tried our best to keep them close to the waterline. Again, we struggled to find decent soil, but the heavy planting bars acted like miniature bulldozers, shoving aside river rocks or crushing them outright whenever we found even the smallest viable patch of mud or silt for the plants to take hold. The sandbar willows came last, and I saved these for a 50-yard-long upstream reach that had lost many shade trees in the flood. The sun now bore down on the streambed unhindered here, and I feared that the water would warm beyond what trout could tolerate.

This stretch proved to be our Burma Road. It was made up of almost entirely newly transported river rocks, so planting felt more like mining. Each willow took minutes of cursing to finally get it into the ground. And the supply seemed never-ending. It felt like I'd plant two, and four more would appear magically in the bucket, ready to be planted. But eventually, with newly formed blisters on our hands, we completed this stretch, too. By now it was late afternoon, and we drove into town for an early supper at the local diner. Never did a burger and a milkshake taste so good.

And on the way back to the cabin, I stopped at a favorite pool on the Delaware as promised. Dark flotsam collecting in the eddies turned out to be rafts of Hendricksons—thousands of them. We scrambled to get on our gear, then made our way down the steep bank with legs already aching from the day's labor. Thankfully, the trout made it easy on us, taking any reasonably cast and imitated dry as they sometimes do early in the season. We each landed three browns before it became too dark to cast. Jim topped off the evening with a long hook-jawed male that jumped three times and measured a full 20 inches. "It was all worth it," he said back at the car, as we peeled off our waders, utterly spent.

I agreed, but there was more to it for me. Before these last six months, beginning when I first staked the willows, what did I know about trees? Sure, I could name some of the more common species, and I appreciated how they shaded the stream. But not until I planted 50 live stakes last October followed by 500 seed-lings on a buggy day in late April did I really come to appreciate them fully. Over the coming weeks and months, I would find myself tree-watching. If I drove past a particularly healthy stand of willows or shrub dogwoods growing along some roadside creek, I would "ooh" and "ah." While fishing, whether it was on the Delaware or another trout stream, I would sometimes find myself turning my back to the river to study what grew along the banks. Did any of this make me a better angler? Probably not, but it did make me regard a trout stream as more than just flowing water, some bugs, and a few fish.

Over the next few months, whenever we pulled into the driveway after the long drive up to the cabin, I would practically explode out of the car to see how "my trees" were doing. Mimi would still be struggling to unbuckle Finn from his car seat, just as I would report back breathlessly, "Willows grew another few inches; dogwoods are starting to leaf out." I began walking the stream—rodless—gazing at my plantings like a farmer admiring his fields. Trees and shrubs had become my surrogate for brookies and rainbows.

And then volunteer seedlings came. One day, I noticed many tiny plants poking up along the high bank of the stream. I picked one of the leaves—no bigger than my pinky nail—and rubbed it between my fingers, then held it up to my nose. It smelled like root beer or, more accurately, birch beer. Birch seedlings—thou-sands of them. I delightedly reported this to Paul, who brought me back to earth when he said, "Think of them like fish eggs. There's thousands of them now, but maybe one in a hundred might make it past a foot."

He was right; enemies of my plantings abounded. Most con-spicuously were the deer that had a penchant for waiting for dog-woods and other shrubs to fully leaf out before gleefully mowing them down. They would arrive like assassins in the night, and I could sometimes hear them from the porch, their sharp hooves clicking and clacking along the stream bottom. Japanese beetles, forest tent caterpillars, and other critters were also more than happy to join the buffet line of succulent new plants. And then there was the town road crew who unknowingly mowed the tops off a dozen spruces literally days after I planted them. I called the highway superintendent and tried not to burst into tears over the phone.

Another threat loomed: invasive species ready to take advantage of postflood conditions, particularly Japanese knotweed. This plant is truly straight out of a science-fiction movie with its ability to regenerate from the smallest speck of live material. Blink, and you're staring at ten feet of it. Cut it down, and eight shoots appear where there was one—the hydra of the plant word. Blink again, and you've got half an acre. It is ubiquitous along the Delaware, where it crowds out native river grasses and destabilizes streambanks. After the flood, I found two knotweed plants attempting to establish themselves. They probably came from upstream, where unfortunately a stand is attempting to muscle its way along the mouth of the pond. I dug each plant up making sure I extracted every electron of root; then I sprayed each hole with a strong weed killer just in case. So far they have not come back.

The stream itself continued to shape and reform. A minor storm would come through and send the water up a few inches. When it receded, pools were deeper. New riffles shoved smaller rocks aside or pushed them downstream, exposing a craggier, fishier-looking bottom. By the end of the summer, I flipped a few rocks and actually saw my first mayfly nymphs. I guessed these recruits came from the upper reaches of the stream, which hadn't received as much flood damage. Hopefully, someday soon, the trout wouldn't be far behind.

By the time we closed the cabin in the fall, the willow stakes had grown a good three feet and looked more like small shrubs rather than sticks. The success of other plantings varied. Some, like the hybrid poplars, had literally taken off, doubling in size to almost six feet tall. Others, like the white spruce and sycamores, did little more than just sit there. The pussy willows varied greatly. Those in direct sun flourished; those in shade languished.

The next season, with the prior year's plantings slowly coming in, I added still more trees courtesy of the state seedling program. This time I ordered, not the mother lode of 500 from the year before, but enough to keep me sweaty and blistered for a weekend. Along with two more riparian packets, I added 25 witch hazel seedlings, a shade-tolerant species I spotted growing in nonchannelized sections of the stream and in the woods behind the cabin. This made it a likely candidate to thrive or at least survive if I planted it. Plus, witch hazel has the fascinating characteristic of flowering in the fall. Not all of my tree purchases were purely for utilitarian purposes.

Then, after this next round was planted, I did something I hadn't considered in nearly two years: I took the two-weight off the pegs from the porch. I knew exactly where I wanted to cast: the culvert pool below the road. I had carefully watched it slowly deepen over the past year. Now it looked downright fishy, with swirling currents and a dark and mysterious bottom.

I knotted on a small barbless Stimulator, stripped off some line, and made a cast from the road. The fly skipped against the current, and I shook the rod tip to dap it like a struggling insect. Then *wham!* Something rocketed from the bottom and grabbed it, hooking itself. This was no time to daintily play a fish, so I joyfully heaved it upward. A six-inch male brook trout, born and raised in the stream, dangled from the Stimulator. I wanted to hug it like the prodigal son come home. Instead I shook it off the hook and watched it plop back into the pool and dart under a boulder.

Given how the stream looked two seasons ago, it felt miraculous that the fish returned. Yet the more I thought about it, not really. Brook trout have been in the Catskills for more than 10,000 years, at least since the massive Wisconsin Glacier receded during the last ice age. Since then, it's a safe assumption that floods far worse than the one in 2006 ravaged the stream. In fact, if the '06 flood was a once-every-700-year event, as the experts say, there have been no fewer than 14 similar-sized storms, not to mention a 1,000-year flood or even a 5,000-year flood. This made me look differently at the stream as a whole. I realized that every streamside boulder, every pool, and every bend could probably be attributed to some calamitous event decades or centuries or even millennia ago. Yet the brookies survived.

On the other hand, the far more insidious threat to brook trout in small streams like mine is the so-called death by a thousand cuts. You know: some siltation from a poorly planned development here, a culvert that blocks fish passage there. Add in some invasive species, take down a few more shade trees to widen the road, and poof: 10,000 years' worth of brook trout have vanished. I remember a friend pointing to a marginal, funky stream in New Jersey near my house and telling me that his grandfather used to catch brookies there in the early 1900s. Today it holds carp and a few pollution-tolerant green sunfish. He used to show off his grandfather's old greenheart fly rod with the name "Lucky Al" hand-painted just above the cork—now just a relic from another time.

This convinced me that more needed to be done to protect the stream. Even with trout beginning to recolonize, something vital was missing: overhead cover. With a greenway of mature trees largely washed away from the banks and then the subsequent clearing of fallen trees by the road crew, there was a dearth of what stream restoration experts called "woody debris." This includes fallen trees, logjams, and the like that provide crucial hiding places to protect trout from predators like herons, mink, and mergansers.

I again spoke with my stream restoration friend from the EPA, and he agreed to come up for a site visit one weekend. He, too, is an angler, so just as I did with Jim, I tempted him with some trout fishing after the work was done. This time, the sulfur hatch on the West Branch should be in full swing.

He brought survey equipment and shot points along certain parts of the stream. He scribbled notes and took pictures. After he finished surveying my quarter-mile of stream, he walked up to the property of my neighbor, who owned a full-half mile above my stretch. More pictures were taken and notes jotted down. He told me he was going to produce a report. He said I might qualify for a U.S. Fish and Wildlife Service program to install some stream-improvement structures.

Ooooh, this sounded good. In my initial research to restore the stream, I came across a booklet showing these devices. They ranged from log cribbings designed to prevent bank erosion while providing overhead cover to channel constrictors—a type of artificial undercut bank that scours the stream bottom deeper to hold more and larger fish. But nearly all of these required heavy equipment, not to mention work crews and state permits, none of which I had.

We unfortunately wound up getting skunked on the West Branch. We floated several miles in my canoe, and sulfurs did indeed come off, but the trout proved to be incredibly selective, ignoring our best attempts to fool them. Still, my friend produced an impressive report, as I knew he would. I tracked down the appropriate contact at the Fish and Wildlife Service and sent him a copy. A few days later, I spoke to him by phone. He said he was definitely interested in funding the work but only for the full three-quarters of a mile of stream. My stretch by itself was too short, so I would need to get permission from my neighbor.

This would be easy, I thought. My neighbor ran the local rod and gun shop in town. I had gotten to know him over the past few years and would stop by from time to time to chat. It would be in his best interest to improve the stream—particularly a nursery that produced rainbow trout that his customers presumably liked to catch. At least that's what I thought.

I mailed him a copy of the report, with a letter explaining the situation and underscoring the part about the nursery aspect of the stream—I believe I used the words *trout factory*. I ended the letter saying I would stop by his store in a few days to discuss the project with him.

The following week, I walked into the shop and was immediately accosted by the new store greeter: a six-month-old beagle pup. By the time the owner walked over to me, I was sitting on the floor scratching the puppy's belly. We exchanged a few pleasantries; then I asked if he had a chance to read the report. He said he did and thought it was very interesting and well done. Thinking all was good, I then asked if he would be interested in participating in the project to restore the stream.

But he shook his head and said no, he was not interested. He explained to me that he did not like the idea of the federal government entering his property. He was a kind man, and I knew he felt empathy with my desire to improve the stream. But he was firm—the feds were not setting foot on his land.

Though we had owned our property for several years now, I was only beginning to understand the distrust of the federal government that ran deep in this rural community. You could see it along roads that bordered the section of the Delaware managed as a National Scenic and Recreation River. Stenciled signs read: "National Park Service Get Out!" The jackbooted thug image was alive and well.

Then he tossed out this thermonuclear bomb: "Plus with all the natural gas drilling about to start around here, who knows what's going to happen."

I looked at him while his words traveled from my ears to my brain. It took another moment for the mushroom cloud to appear in my mind.

I sputtered, "Wait—what?"

May 20: It's almost dark now, and trout have finally begun to come up steadily. For the past 90 minutes in this broad Delaware River glide, fish rose sporadically, and just a scattering of bugs hatched. But with the sun now set and nighthawks swooping and barrel-rolling in the twilight above me, mayfly spinners have begun falling.

On the far side of the glide, well beyond casting range, several trout have set up and are noisily gulping down spinners. But there's no way I can reach them. Each time a particularly large fish comes up, I find myself muttering a low, guttural "ooof," like I've been punched in the stomach.

But then trout begin rising closer to me. The rise forms are subtle and hard to see in this confused, black water. Sometimes just a bubble or two is the only tip-off that anything happened. I spot a pair coming up side by side some 30 feet away. I cast to them. But the currents are complicated. It seems that each time my fly drifts close to a fish, some microeddy boils up and drags it unnaturally. I try throwing my best slack-line casts and mending fly line but still no takers. Eventually, the trout move downstream—probably as punishment for my poor presentation.

Then a fish comes up close to me but in an even harder spot: on the far side of a narrow eddy below a submerged boulder. Currents battle against each other here, forming a distinct rip-line of fast and slow water. Cast here, and line and leader will immediately get pulled in opposite directions, and the fly will drag across the surface like a water-skier.

Still, I want to see how close I can get to this fish, so I shuffle a few feet each time it rises. Eventually, I'm just ten feet away in waist-deep water just on this side of the submerged boulder. But I know if I cast, my fly will immediately drag and potentially put down the fish. I stand frustrated as eddies swirl around me. The trout might as well be on the other side of the river with the noisy gulpers. It comes up and takes another spinner. Ooof.

I consider my options. The first thing I do is change my fly. The low-floating Rusty Spinner I had been using is drowned and waterlogged anyway, so I clip it off and stick it to the dry patch on my vest. Then I turn my back to the fish, click on my headlamp, and open a fly box. I peruse rows and rows of dries and select an underrated sleeper: The Usual. It is thoroughly ugly, with a wing and tail of bushy snowshoe hair and a brownish-red body. A well-tied one lays on the river off-keel like a swamped sailboat. It looks like nothing—yet everything.

I knot it to my tippet and wait for the fish to rise again. It does. Then I decide to try something different. Instead of casting, I simply hold the rod high and outward and let the fly gently drop inches upstream of the fish. It lands gently, and I jiggle the rod ever so slightly, bringing the usual to life.

The fly is immediately sucked down. I come tight, and a huge trout catapults wildly away from me. One word flashes in my mind: beast. *It crashes back in and tears to the far side of the river. As it runs, my reel, an ancient Scientific Anglers, scratched and dinged to bare steel in some spots, makes an angry, high-pitched noise, reminding me that I really ought to spray it with WD-40 one of these seasons.*

The trout stops somewhere out there, and all I can do is hold tight. For a few moments I savor that I am once again connected literally and figuratively to this wild trout river. It's as if the entire Delaware and the surrounding mountains and forests have been rendered and purified into this single trout, and I have been allowed to briefly mainline into all of it. It's the closest feeling I can get to flying.

That is, if I can land this fish. If I don't, if I snap it off or the hook somehow pulls, I will feel more like Icarus, who flew too close to the sun and plummeted back to earth and drowned.

The trout breaks the spell with powerful head shakes, followed by another crazed run. It stops, and I begin backing toward the shoreline, slowly gaining line on the reel, turn by turn. The fish boils in front of me, and I can see its dorsal and tail break the surface. They are delightfully far apart.

A few minutes later, the fish is on its side at my feet in two inches of water. I kneel down and click on my headlamp. It takes up virtually the entire beam of light—a dusky brown trout tastefully spotted head to tail and with blueish hues around its cheeks. I quickly measure it at 19 inches long. I reach past rows of teeth and extract the bedraggled Usual from the roof of its mouth. Then I point the fish into the current and hold it, allowing it to regain its strength. In the cold water, it feels particularly hard-bodied and strong.

Then I think about the technique I just used to hook this fish—dapping the fly instead of casting it—and how I perfected it on the six-foot-wide stream. There it catches scale-model brookies and rainbows. Here on the big river, it fooled a brown that would consider those fish a light snack.

Then, as I do in both waters, I ease my grip and watch the trout shoot away.

The Joys of Fishing
and Fracking

Let's go back to a few years before we bought our cabin—390 million to be exact. It was the early Devonian period, more than 150 million years before the first dinosaurs roamed. Terrestrial earth consisted of just two primary landmasses: Gondwana in the Southern Hemisphere and Euramerica to the North. The first vascular plants, including ferns and horsetails, were busy forming the world's earliest forests.

Great seas covered the rest of the planet, and they ran thick with fish—so much so, the Devonian is also known as the "Age of Fishes." Some of the earliest forms of sharks and rays swam with placoderms—a now-extinct group of armored fish with jaws of beak-like bony blades they used instead of teeth. Lobe-finned fishes abounded, too, and their decedents would crawl ashore as the precursors to the first amphibians. All are extinct now, except for the coelacanth—a Devonian holdout rediscovered alive and well during a fishing expedition off South Africa in 1938.

Throughout the Age of Fishes, the Catskills, along with parts of Pennsylvania, West Virginia, and Ohio, were covered in a vast, shallow sea. Over eons, algae and plankton and presumably fish died, sank to the bottom, and accumulated. Eventually they were covered over by layers of sediment.

Then landmasses shifted, oceans retreated, and tectonic plates collided. Some lands heaved upward, forming the Himalaya-like

early Catskills. Others were forced downward, trapping immense quantities of organic material miles below the surface.

And that is where this story begins.

Just before we entered into contract to buy the cabin, the seller's son, Joe, mailed me a file folder. Inside were two deeds: one for a right of way, allowing me to access my driveway (Tim technically owns a narrow strip of land bordering the road), and the other for three acres on the far side of the stream acquired in the 1980s to ensure privacy.

But there was something else in the folder: a one-page signed lease to the Atlantic Richfield Company, better known as ARCO (today owned by energy leviathan BP). Best as I could tell, the lease gave ARCO the right to explore for oil and gas on the property.

I was thoroughly confused. Oil and gas? Here? In this land of quiet forests and streams? This wasn't Texas or on the North Slope of Alaska, so I asked the attorney working on our closing to please investigate.

It was legitimate, it turned out. The attorney explained that, years ago, some energy companies considered this region of the

Catskills potentially rich in fossil fuels due to its geology. They approached landowners and offered them leases for a few dollars per acre. Most happily signed, looking at their offers as free money with the idea that it would probably never come to pass. And it hadn't up to that point.

Then I asked if the lease was still valid. The attorney told me no, it had expired years ago. I remember saying, "Good, because if there was an active lease to drill here, there is no way I'd want to buy the place." And then I promptly forgot all about it.

But those early leases came before energy companies developed something called high-volume horizontal hydraulic fracturing, also known as fracking. Here's the oversimplified version of how fracking works: You drill a hole vertically into the ground, then turn the bit sideways, and drill some more. Then you pump water and fluids into the hole at high pressure to fracture shale lying deep below the surface. The shale contains pockets of natural gas or oil, which come bubbling up.

Fracking quickly revolutionized the energy industry. By drilling horizontally, gas and oil companies could tap reserves previously thought inaccessible due to their extreme depths. This included places like the Barnett Shale in Texas, Bakken Shale in North Dakota, and something called the Marcellus Shale—an enormous natural gas field from the Devonian period lying in an extinct seabed a mile beneath, you guessed it, our cabin.

By 2007, in Pennsylvania, fracking in the Marcellus Shale had already begun, and it quickly developed into a full-blown land rush. Owners of hardscrabble farms, barely holding on a few years earlier, signed lucrative leases for thousands of dollars per acre, not to mention royalties for any gas extracted from underneath their land. Gas wells sprung up next to cornfields, forests, even schools. Sleepy villages awoke and boomed. The U.S. Geological Survey estimated that the Marcellus may hold hundreds of trillions of cubic feet of gas reserves. The CEO of one of the energy companies started calling the United States and its shale deposits the "Saudi Arabia of natural gas." A tsunami was headed our way.

First, I started hearing about "landmen"—agents of the gas companies—combing the local countryside, vying to secure leases from property owners. Many were successful, and I learned that several neighbors had quickly signed on. Shortly after that, I received my first offer in the mail for $1,000 per acre plus royalties. Then a higher offer came in, one that would have essentially paid off the rest of the mortgage for the cabin. Just sign right here on the dotted line.

Of course, there was a flip side to fracking. Where to begin? Let's start with the fluids used in the fracking process. The gas companies often benignly referred to them as "water and additives." But what additives? And here is where it quickly started to get scary. One website I found stated that a menu of as many as 600 chemicals could be used, depending on the type of well. Some were known carcinogens, such as benzene. Energy companies would respond to these concerns by pointing out that many of the same chemicals they used in fracking fluids were, as they liked to put it, "found in the same products you might find under your own kitchen sink." They would say this as if we all start our day with a nice hot cup of Drāno.

Then they would say the well casings were reinforced with cement and steel, with virtually no chance they would ever crack and leak fracking fluids or natural gas into groundwater. No chance. Never will happen. Not in a thousand years. I thought about the legacy left behind from the coal industry in Pennsylvania, where acid mine drainage had laid waste to literally thousands of miles of streams. In one of my favorite fishing books, *Trout Streams of Pennsylvania*, author Dwight Landis makes multiple references to waterways that are outright dead zones due to acid mine drainage—devoid of so much as a mosquito larvae, let alone a trout. Did the long-gone owners of the coal companies know or understand the impacts their mines would have all these years later?

Again, the gas companies would counter, saying that the fracking fluids remained a mile below the surface, entombed under layer after layer of rock and strata. How could they possibly make it to the surface? This seemed like a logical argument until I read a report prepared by the city of New York concerned with fracking near upstate watershed lands that safeguard city-owned reservoirs. In the report, geologists cited the possibility of preexisting faults in shale acting as conduits to deliver fracking fluids many miles from a well site. Where would they go? An aquifer? A river? The six-foot-wide stream? No one knew.

Then I began reading news stories of landowners in Pennsylvania reporting fouled drinking water shortly after fracking began in their communities. The energy companies claimed the contamination had taken place before fracking—a preexisting condition. But the landowners said otherwise, holding up plastic water jugs full of an opaque brownish brew they said came from their taps. Around that time, a documentary about fracking called *Gasland* had come out. It showed a man actually light his tap water on fire.

And that's when I found out that one of the first high-volume horizontal hydraulic fracturing wells being planned for the state of New York was to be sited a few thousand feet from my cabin. I could walk to it in three minutes. All I'd have to do is cross the culvert and head down the dirt road that parallels the six-foot-wide stream, then hang a left to the planned site of the well pad. Or pretty soon I could just follow all the trucks carrying fracking fluid.

With apologies to Humphrey Bogart in *Casablanca*, of all the trout streams in all the towns in all the world, fracking walks into mine.

It turned out that our cabin was to be included in something called a "spacing unit," a one-square-mile block of land drawn up by the state, where multiple horizontal wells would be drilled. This particular application called for six of them, and at least one would go directly under my property. As a landowner, there was nothing I could do about it. You see, in New York State, there is something called "compulsory integration," a rule that says if enough of the surrounding landowners want drilling under their properties, it will happen under yours, too, whether you want it or not. The letter from the state's Division of Mineral Resources made it seem like I had won the lottery. According to the paperwork they sent me, all I'd have to do is pretty much just sit back and collect the royalties. But to my mind, it smacked of eminent domain driven by the energy companies. Shortly after the state wrote me, I started receiving strange letters from land speculators, congratulating me on my good fortune and wanting to talk to me about forming some sort of partnership.

This was all deeply troubling. How could fracking possibly be compatible with the woodlands around me or the six-foot-wide stream or the greater Catskills landscape? A fracking operation is nothing less than a not-so-small industrial complex. I had seen images of fully operational fracking wells, and they looked as benign as an aircraft carrier dropped in the middle of a forest or field. To build one, first of all, you need trucks, and lots of them. I calculated that, with the 5 to 8 million gallons of water plus fluids needed to frack each well, not to mention construction equipment to build the initial well pad, the road in front of my cabin was about to become the New Jersey Turnpike. And all of those trucks would have to wend their way down a serpentine dirt road with no guard rails that turns greasy-slick whenever it rains. And yes, this was the same dirt road that washed away three times in as many years.

Along with the endless truck trips, there would be clear-cutting, digging an artificial pond to hold water and fluids, the earthquake-like sound of the actual fracking, flaring of wells that would look like a supernova, and of course the coming and going of humanity in an area where rush hour currently consisted of two pickups per hour instead of one. And it wouldn't just be noisy, bright, and smelly to me. I found a study by the Wildlife

Conservation Society that listed bird species particularly sensitive to human disturbance. They included black-throated green warblers, hermit thrushes, ovenbirds, scarlet tanagers, and winter wrens—all of which currently nested in the woods behind the cabin.

Back to water. Where would it all come from? No, not the stream, thank God, which was too small for the millions of gallons needed, but probably from one of the nearby branches of the Delaware. This was problematic, too. Each summer, the Delaware seemed perpetually starved of much of its flow by an always-thirsty New York City, which diverts a significant proportion of the river's water through a series of underground aqueducts. Now a giant straw was about to come in and suck up some more. And they wouldn't just drink it; they would also lace it with contaminants and pump it a mile below the surface. Some of the wastewater would come back to the surface, where it would have to be disposed of, even though no local treatment plants were currently prepared to handle what essentially was toxic waste. Some of the waste would even contain radioactive materials brought up from the shale itself.

Yes, the prospect of fracking was enough to keep you up at night. And it did.

Meanwhile, ironically, the stream looked better and better with each passing month. The willow stakes had grown to six feet or taller, and many of the other plantings and volunteer seedlings flourished. The streambed continued to reengineer itself, and the trout responded in kind, taking up lies in new pools and runs. I could take my two-weight once again and raise trout almost at will if conditions were right. Yet other times I would just sit on my porch overlooking the stream and lament, imagining the thousands of trucks endlessly lumbering and Jake-braking past. Or I'd see a truck filled with fracking fluids careening off the road in slow motion and landing headlong into the stream.

I found myself writing letters and attending public hearings. I became a reluctant activist. This was not easy because I knew many of my neighbors had signed leases and welcomed energy development on their land. And I couldn't blame or fault them for signing, particularly those who lived here year-round. Beyond my bucolic cabin and little stream, people struggled here—particularly in the bleak winter months, when I was back home in suburban New Jersey. I knew, as the saying goes, that you can't eat the scenery. The people who signed leases wanted to trust that fracking was perfectly safe and that state regulations would protect them. I couldn't make that leap.

I spoke to one landowner troubled over what to do. He owned a second home on more than 40 acres and truly loved his land. But he remained conflicted. He was well off and didn't need the money, but he believed that allowing the gas companies to drill might be the right thing to do. He saw it as almost a duty to harvest a domestic energy source that would be used for the public good. But in the end, probably giving in to pressures from friends and family, he didn't sign. And I believe it gnawed at him. Other second-home-owners were far more mercenary, leasing their land in the hopes of a big cash payout.

And then there was Tim, who didn't sign. His logic for not doing so was sound: "So I'd get a check and buy a truck," he told me. "But what good's a truck if I can't drink my water? And then the truck will rust out anyway, and I still can't drink the water." It should be noted that Tim has a spring on his property that produces the finest-tasting water I have ever put to my lips. It's tucked in a low spot beneath a dark hemlock grove. It always smells dewy and wonderful in there. The water gushes from a pipe that empties into a shallow pool full of green watercress. It's toothachingly cold, and when you drink it on a hot day, you can feel it immediately air-condition your body as it travels from your mouth downward.

A landman representing one of the larger gas companies proved to be particularly relentless with Mimi and me. He left messages on our home phone several times that we always ignored.

He sent multiple ready-to-sign leases, which we promptly tossed into the recycling bin. One day we had just returned to New Jersey from upstate, and a neighbor told us someone had stopped by looking for us. He left a card, and I immediately recognized the name. So I decided to finally call him. When I got him on the phone, he said that he "happened to be in the neighborhood" and decided to drop by. Then he laughed and admitted his office was currently in the town near my cabin 125 miles away. I could tell I had a true salesman on the line, the kind who would have you driving away in a brand-new car when all you wanted was an oil change. But my armor was well fastened that day.

The conversation went like this:

"So, did you have a chance to look at our offer?"

"Yes."

"Well what did you think?"

"I'm not interested."

"It's a generous offer."

"I'm not interested."

"Is there some sort of environmental concern?"

"Not interested."

"Are there any other concerns?"

What I wanted to say was this: "Speaking on behalf of the brook trout, rainbows, mayflies, stoneflies, salamanders, frogs, toads, peepers, newts, and assorted thrushes, warblers, and flycatchers currently under my stewardship, I am declining your offer."

But instead, I said once again, "Not interested."

The landman paused. I felt like a turtle safely tucked in its shell with a coyote circling, trying to use all of its wits and guile to find an opening. I remained clamped shut.

Then he said if I changed my mind to please call him, and he hung up.

Right around then, drilling permits were delayed, pending comments to the New York Department of Environmental Conservation's (DEC) newly issued *Supplemental Generic Environ-*

mental Impact Statement, a 1,000-page tome of drilling regulations for the new wells, including the one down the road from me.

But by now, a full-fledged movement emerged against fracking. The negative connection between drinking water and gas extraction had cemented, even after the DEC announced that it would not allow it on watershed lands or "primary aquifers." Lands not in those categories were rightfully dubbed "sacrifice zones" by fracking opponents. Environmental groups, from the new but rapidly strengthening Catskill Mountainkeeper to more established organizations like Trout Unlimited, organized small armies.

Public hearings grew rowdy. When a commercial river outfitter testified in favor of fracking, stating he actually believed it would be good for tourism because people would want to come out and see the wells, boos rained down like thunder. It turned out he had already leased hundreds of acres hoping for a cash payout. Those against fracking repeated over and over the term *cumulative impacts* in their testimony. They wanted the DEC to address, not the impact of one well, but the many thousand impacts that would invariable arise after the first were permitted. Eventually the DEC would go on to receive a quarter-million comments from the public.

More news came out about fracking, and much of it was bad. A peer-reviewed study confirmed methane migration into drinking water from shoddy well construction. A pipe ruptured at a fracking site in Pennsylvania, sending thousands of gallons of wastewater laced with fracking fluids and salts into a tributary of a popular trout stream. Reports came out documenting thousands of violations racked up by gas companies in Pennsylvania. These ranged from minor spills and leaks to improper waste disposal. Fracking proponents would claim these violations showed that the state was properly doing its job to regulate the industry and enforce laws. My guess is that none of these violations happened on their own property or favorite stream. To my mind, each violation was just another example of death by a thousand cuts.

But billions of dollars were undeniably being made in Pennsylvania, not to mention tax revenues. Despite various environmental concerns, the fight against fracking began to feel like standing in the way of a locomotive. Stories circulated that New York's decision was imminent. I tried to rationalize that maybe gas royalties would make up for the loss of the cabin's birds and fish. But it didn't work, as I remained unclear on how exactly does one put a price on a hermit thrush or a school of fingerling rainbows.

Then, on December 17, 2014, Christmas came gloriously early. At a cabinet meeting in Albany that day, Governor Andrew Cuomo made his decision on whether to allow high-volume horizontal hydraulic fracturing in New York State. He turned the microphone over to his health commissioner Howard Zucker, who said, "Would I live in a community with (fracking) based on the facts I have now? Would I let my child play in a school field nearby or my family drink the water from the tap or grow vegetables in the soil? After looking at the plethora of reports . . . my answer is no."

When I was in the sixth grade, I asked for a four-lane Aurora slot-car racing set for Christmas. I knew it was expensive, and there was virtually no chance that my parents would actually buy it for me. But in the days running up to the holiday, it was fun to at least imagine my friends and me having raucous races and rallies. Then Christmas morning came, and I opened a large gift-wrapped box underneath the tree. There it was, gleaming like a giant bar of gold: the Aurora four-lane slot-car set—the greatest Christmas present I ever received. Until this one.

I read the headline of the *New York Times* on my computer over and over: "Citing Health Risks, Cuomo Bans Fracking in New York State." I wanted to make sure it was real. It was. I closed the door in my office. The past several years of hearings, letters, rallies, and worries came rushing back. Then I called Mimi, and I heard my voice crack when I told her what had just happened. A rally erupted in front of the governor's office in Manhattan that afternoon, and to this day, I regret not going. If I ever meet the man, I will hug him.

Yet at the same time, I knew many of my neighbors upstate were saddened by the news. But I also knew those who signed leases received some sort of signing bonus, which they would get to keep. I hoped they would look at it like found money, like those early leases from decades ago. As for me, soon it would be time to go fishing again.

The next spring, I waded the stream in early May, casting here and there. Trout rose greedily. The plantings had become a chartreuse tunnel of new growth. The woods dripped with migratory birds. All seemed well.

But I knew that, a mile underneath me, the gas was still there—the ancient legacy from the Age of Fishes (and yes, the irony is not lost on me). And though fracking is currently banned in the Catskills, I know gas companies still lustfully gaze at the region, particularly areas surrounding the Delaware River watershed. I've come to think of it like the next big flood: It might come, it might not, but I will need to stay vigilant. As conservationist George Schaller once wrote, "There are never victories in conservation. If you want to save a species or a habitat, it's a fight forevermore. You can never turn your back."

And I won't. But in the meantime, the trout are rising, and I will cast for them.

May 25: The spot is full of poison ivy. And ticks. And timber rattlesnakes. So don't go there. Ever. Plus, it's not particularly fun to fish—a steep, uneven shoreline where you have to stand angularly, like you are wearing high heels instead of waders. One wrong step, and you are in cold river water up to your chin. But trout like to line up in the bubble line just off the bank and eat sulfurs. So here I am.

The fish gently tilts up once every 30 seconds and takes another bug. I approach it from upriver, where I plan to float my fly down to it. This runs counter to traditional fly fishing dogma, which says to cast a dry fly upstream only. But here on the big river, if you want to consistently hook trout, you feed the fly downstream and hopefully into the fish's mouth.

But there's a problem: I have to get into casting position first without spooking the fish, which more or less is looking directly at me. This is particularly challenging because I'm perched relatively high up on this steep bank with nowhere else to go. So I crouch so low I am practically crawling—poison ivy and ticks be damned. Meanwhile the trout continues to rise steadily.

I inch along until I reach a spot where I'm close enough to make a reasonable cast. But instead of staying on my knees, I decide to sit in the grass, slowly swing my legs out, and let them dangle over the riverbank. I do so, and my only direct connection to the water are the bottoms of my boots, now resting against a partially submerged rock. If I had a cane pole, I might look like Huck Finn dunking worms for catfish.

The trout comes up again maybe 30 feet away. I look over my shoulder to calculate the physics of how to keep the fly and leader from snagging in the steep brushy bank behind me. I angle my back cast upward, then manage a sort of half-roll cast up and out into the river. It's ugly, but it somehow works.

The first few casts are off the mark, but the next one is not. It lands six feet above the trout and maybe three feet beyond its feeding lane, which is my intention. I quickly lift the rod to skip the fly up current and above the fish. Then I drop the tip and pop a few extra feet of slack into the river so the fly can drift without drag.

It works, and I tense while my sulfur imitation approaches the trout. It drifts another foot, then pushes up in a bulge of water and vanishes in a slow, confident rise. I lift the rod and feel solid, thumping weight. Then the fish very purposefully turns and heads into the current and downstream. This is not the high-octane run of a crazed rainbow just before it greyhounds out of the water. It is the measured but unstoppable retreat of a very big brown that has just declared,

"I don't like this, and I am going home to my favorite logjam three miles downriver."

Fly line pours off the reel in one, long, sustained run. First, the thicker weight-forward section is gone, followed by the thinner running line. Then I feel a little speed bump of my backing knot dancing through the guides, chased by yards of thin, white Dacron.

I try to stay calm, and I do this by remaining seated. The grassy bank has become my fighting chair. My feet are braced on the rock, and the deeply bent nine-foot five-weight is pointed upward, with the butt resting firmly against my belly as if in a gimbal on a rod belt.

All I can do is wait for the fish to stop running. When it finally does, it immediately changes course and begins swimming toward me. I reel quickly but steadily to keep even pressure on the rod. I don't want any sudden movements to agitate this fish any further. I don't want it to jump, and I don't want it to run again. I want to gently but firmly ease it closer and closer, until, before it realizes what has happened, this trout of a lifetime is in my hands.

Yes, I believed it was that big.

Reeling up 50 feet of backing plus an entire 90 feet of fly line takes a long time even without an enormous trout on the other end. Minutes pass, and the fish slowly draws closer. The backing knot comes bumping back up the rod—briefly catching on one of the snake guides and terrifying me—but then pulls free and safely nestles back onto the reel. Then comes the running line and the first half of the weight-forward head.

I strain to see the fish, which up to this point is just an unseen force. How big is it? I have heard stories of 25- and 26-inch browns sometimes taken. A few years earlier, there were rumors of a 10-pound, 30-incher caught in the West Branch maybe 15 miles from where I stand—I mean sit.

Just then I see it—a yellow flash 15 feet away and maybe 4 feet deep. But that's all it is: a flash. Too far and too vague for me to even begin to estimate its size. And by now, that's all I want, just a good look to know if it's four pounds or five pounds or maybe even larger.

I'm sweating now. All it will take is another few turns of line on the reel to get my first solid glimpse, and I will know.

And then, without warning, it's gone.

The hook has pulled. Just like that.

The rod hangs limp as I reel up the last few feet of fly line. The sulfur imitation comes to the surface and V-wakes in the current, looking like a wet piece of fuzz after being submerged for the last 10 minutes.

The full gravity of what just happened sinks in—that I will never see this trout. Ever. And it will haunt me. I slump in my grassy fighting chair feeling like Hemingway losing a 1,000-pound marlin off Cuba.

The big river flows past, oblivious. Sulfurs continue to hatch.

Eventually it's time to get up and look for more risers while dodging ticks, poison ivy, and rattlesnakes. Like I said, you don't ever want to go to this wicked place.

My Beautiful Outhouse

With fracking blown up like the Death Star, and the Empire hopefully not striking back anytime soon, it was time to divert my energies to other things. Like sewage.

Right after we bought the cabin, one of the very first repairs we needed to make was to the waste line leading from the toilet into the ground. The old cast-iron pipe had cracked, and every time you flushed, some water leaked onto the ground underneath the cabin. Yes, it was disgusting.

So a plumber friend from New Jersey offered to come up to make the repair. He wasn't an angler, so I couldn't bribe him with my usual promise of mayfly hatches and rising trout. But he did like to drink a beer or two, so he agreed to make a long-distance house call in exchange for a couple of cases. Like I said, he was a friend.

He climbed partway underneath the cabin and, with just his legs showing, began the job of removing the old pipe, replacing it with PVC that would last indefinitely. I sat on the ground and passed tools like a nurse assisting a surgeon.

Over the sound of hacksawing and hammering, I asked him, "By the way, where does the sewage go?"

"No idea," he said, just as he handed me the offending hunk of cracked iron.

Mimi remembers the owner's son at least mentioning sewage, but I can't recall the conversation. Knowing my usual flea-like

attention span for home-improvement talk, it probably went something like this:

Joe: " . . . and so that's where the sewage goes. Any questions?"

Me: "So rainbows and brookies in the stream, right?"

From what Mimi recollects, Joe didn't really know exactly where it went either. She said he gestured somewhere in the backyard and said that there might be a septic or a cesspool or something.

I remember asking Tim once because he's lived up the road from the cabin his entire life. He recalled someone digging a hole in the ground and installing "some sort of box." Again, not a lot to go on.

But the toilet did flush, and its contents did go down the waste pipe without any trouble. And because I have never seen bits of toilet paper or other unmentionables bobbing down the stream alongside mayflies or caddis, I'm still going by the assumption that everything is jake down there, and I'd like to keep it that way.

Managing water—whether going out or coming in—has always been interesting at the cabin. The morning after we closed, I tried turning on the tap, and nothing happened. I did pay attention to Joe enough to know that there was no well, that the water came from a spring, but that's all I knew. So I peered underneath the cabin and could see the detached waterline in the form of a black plastic pipe poking up from the ground coming from the general direction of the shed. So I walked an imaginary line until the pipe reemerged near the edge of the woods and continued along the stream above ground. I followed it until it ended 50 yards upstream at a large, stainless steel tank set into the base of a steep hill running along the stream. A notch in the topography there revealed a wet, spongy seep. A spring. Next to the steel tank, a length of black, plastic pipe stuck out of the ground, and water ran from it. Various other lengths of pipe laid scattered about, and the whole system had a kind of Rube Goldberg feel to it.

After a trip to the hardware store to buy new pipe, fittings, hose clamps, and a propane blowtorch to connect them, I began piecing the system back together. I replaced broken pipe and cracked connectors. Then I scrubbed out the tank and reconnected the intake pipe. Water flowed in. When the tank filled, I turned on the reconnected waterline that entered the cabin. At first it gurgled and spat as air and pockets of water pushed out. And then, finally, water; clear, pure spring water flowed freely. The project wound up taking up most of the morning when I could have been fishing, but it felt good, like I was Jeremiah Johnson. Cabin's got good water. Yes sir, good water.

But the system wasn't perfect. The cabin sat at a lower elevation than the spring, and water pressure relied on gravity. This worked fine for everything except the shower, which ran from a hose coming from the wall around waist high. This looked strange when I first noticed it, and I quickly found out why it was so oddly positioned. If I held the shower head any higher than my navel, no water came out, as you now apparently exceeded the elevation of the spring. To fix this problem, I bought a battery-powered shower for camping and would fill a bucket directly from the faucet in the tub. More Rube Goldberg, but it worked.

And to those who might say, "Why didn't you just drill a well or buy a large holding tank and use a jet pump to fill it or something else that would require more than $25 worth of plastic pipe and assorted hardware," I say this: "Remember, it's a *cabin*."

It all became moot after the '06 flood, which destroyed most of the system. It tore out all of the pipe upstream of the shed and buried the holding tank in rock and debris. I suppose I could have excavated it out and started over, but I had already been eyeballing another spring I had discovered. This one sat high above the stream on a shaded plateau in the woods. An ancient-looking concrete foundation lined it, so it had obviously been used at one point. But the foundation had created a sort of frog pond clogged with silt and mud, so I took a sledgehammer to it, smashing it open and draining it to locate the actual source. After it emptied, I discovered a single stream of water flowing over gravel, deliciously clear and cold, from underneath a large rock.

I bought a 60-gallon plastic holding tank and set it in the ground on a slightly lower spot than the spring. I stacked rocks on the outside to camouflage it. Who wants to see a piece of plastic in the woods? This was followed by another trip to the hardware store to buy more pipe, fittings, and clamps. I ran a pipe from under the rock and into the tank, which in turn drained through an outlet pipe. Then it flowed down the hill and into the cabin.

And this time, I had enough water pressure to take a shower standing luxuriously upright. It is a cabin, but we're not Neanderthals, either.

The system continues to be nearly foolproof except on exceptionally dry summers, when the spring slows to a near trickle. Then water has to be stingily conserved and showers replaced with swims in the Delaware or dips in the six-foot-wide stream.

Note I said *nearly* foolproof. You see there was this one incident . . .

When I first hooked up the new spring and placed the pipe underneath the rock at the source, I didn't see the need to screen it. I mean, what could possibly get in there? Then a few weeks later, during one of the aforementioned luxurious showers, I noticed an odor coming from the water. It was the smell of decay. I wasn't sure what to make of it, so I ignored it, hoping it would go away.

Then later that day when Mimi was using the kitchen sink, the water stopped altogether. We tried other sinks, but nothing was flowing. So I, the new master of all things having to do with the spring, announced I would fix it. I bounded up the hillside to troubleshoot the problem. I began at the intake pipe. All clear there, and the tank was full, so I began working my way toward the cabin. Each time I undid a length of pipe to check, water flowed unfettered. Eventually I wound up back at the cabin and realized that the problem must be from one of the pipes underneath it. So like my plumber friend, I shimmied beneath and found myself lying on the ground on my back with just my legs sticking out.

It was close under there. The waterline led to a connector, where two pipes branched off. I detached the first one, and water flowed from it, indicating no clog. But when I opened the second, nothing came out. Mimi was directly overhead in the kitchen. I called up to her, "I think I found the clog."

I shimmied closer to the clogged pipe and tried to clear it by blowing into it. Nothing happened, so then I decided maybe I should try the reverse and suck out whatever was in there.

I exhaled, put the pipe to my mouth, and inhaled sharply. The clog cleared immediately—directly into my mouth. But it wasn't some pebbles or clot of dead leaves I had anticipated. Instead, it was a six-inch dead, rotted, bloated spring salamander along with a shot-glass full of fetid water. I writhed and gagged, trying to pry myself from under the cabin so I could sit up and spit out this most devilish of nature's practical jokes. Mimi ran from the back door to see what had happened. All she had heard was something that sounded like a backed-up sink and then the thrashing of arms and legs.

By now I had wriggled out and was coughing and gagging and pointing to the pinkish blob of decayed flesh on the ground beside me. Later that day, I fit a heavy-gauge screen over the intake pipe, where it's remained ever since.

Let's go back to sewage. Twice a year I have get-togethers at the cabin with up to ten friends and fishing buddies staying over long weekends. Now the unwritten rule has always been that, for gentlemen, the nearest tree would suffice for—let me assume we are all mature here—number one. But for number two, the credo has been *mi baño es su baño*.

The first few years went fine, and in fact, I am happy to report there have never been any outright disasters. We never had to call the now-defunct pump-out service I used to see locally advertised called Stinky Steve's. But at some point, I began to worry about this semiannual tectonic movement of poo. So I began to encourage the more adventuresome in the group to fully explore my 14 acres with trowel in hand. The only rule was to stay below the elevation of the spring. This seemed to work fine for my more-woodsy friends, but it was unacceptable for others who were less in tune with their inner bear-in-the-woods. For those sophisticates, I needed to rent a Porta Potty. But I realized that neither solution was truly sustainable.

That's when I began to consider a third option: an outhouse. Ironically, there happened to already be one right on the premises. When I first opened up the shed after we bought the place, I noticed that the inside seemed smaller than its actual footprint. So I wandered around to the back and found a second door. I opened it slowly. It made a low creaking sound. Craning my neck, I peered inside and saw what looked like a haunted house. Spiderwebs draped around a one-hole bench. Mouse nests poked out from all corners and hung from rafters. A few cave crickets stared back at me. One of them fled by jumping directly down the hole. I slammed the door and don't believe I've opened it since. But more importantly, the outhouse sat far too close to the stream. And though I knew a certain amount of organic nutrients can actually help bolster mayfly hatches, leachate from human waste was not the way to go.

So I decided to site, design, and build an entirely new structure. I consulted with friends, who all loved the idea. Many offered to help. I found plans online, but the estimated cost of materials alone ran over $1,000. And then there was the actual hole in the ground—sometimes called the "honey hole." Knowing the amount of rocks that lay just under the surface, how in God's name would I dig a four-foot-by-four-foot-deep hole? Hire an excavator? Like many projects, the gap between theory and actual execution remained light-years apart.

I found myself researching alternative toilets. They ranged from extremely rudimentary—a spackle bucket lined with a plastic bag—to expensive incinerating systems with propane lines that flambé one's feces into harmless ash. None seemed like the right way to go.

Then I discovered online a manual developed by Vermont's Green Mountain Club on something called a "moldering privy." The manual described it as "having great promise for disposal of human wastes in the back country." Do tell. I learned that a moldering privy was essentially an outhouse that relied on "cold composting," or moldering, to break down human waste. Your typical compost pile relies on "hot composting," which requires frequent turning of the pile to keep things aerated and moving along, so to speak. This is why you sometimes see compost piles giving off steam—they actually produce heat in the decomposition process.

Not so with moldering. The secret was adding two key ingredients: the first was something called "forest duff"—the layer of partially decomposed leaves on the forest floor. Apparently, duff contains all sorts of tiny composting critters eager to do nature's dirty work. So the first step to moldering is to line the bottom of your pile with a healthy duff layer. After that, you top off each "deposit" with a handful, or scoop, of duff (and yes, aim counts). Then the little guys have at it. The other secret ingredient is the manure worm, or red wiggler, which you add to the pile at the beginning of the season. They, too, join in on the banquet. A thousand cost around $30 online. And best of all, I learned there was no pit to dig. The pile, so to speak, remains suspended off the ground in a wooden cribbing lined with mesh, with the outhouse sitting above it. This allows air to penetrate from all sides, which apparently is a key to good moldering. Moisture, the other essential element, comes from urine. Between the duff, wigglers, air exposure, and moisture, composting occurs fairly quickly and with little to no odor. Eventually the cribbing would fill, and a new one would need to be built, but in a lightly used loo like mine, that would take years.

By the way, most traditional outhouses do not compost at all. In a deep pit, wastes are not exposed to enough moisture or air circulation to fully break down. In fact, some hardcore antique hunters seek out the long-closed pits of 100-year-old outhouses to excavate piles of poop for such buried treasure as old bottles (outhouses were frequently used as garbage cans, too). They report that the contents of the piles, while inert, are surprisingly well-preserved. Gross!

Speaking of outhouses, I still needed one, so I took a chance and started searching online and was surprisingly rewarded for my efforts almost immediately. I found a guy who lived about 100 miles away who built them from scrap wood he buys at auctions. They looked solid, framed out of pine and sheathed-in planks of beadboard, with a vented metal roof. And the price was right: $250. So I bribed a nephew who attended a nearby college to strap it to the back of his pickup and deliver it. He is a deer hunter, so in exchange, I told him he could erect a tree stand wherever he chose on the property (he picked a good spot, apparently, and now shoots a doe or two each year).

He showed up at the cabin with the outhouse, along with three of his college buddies still laughing at all of the strange looks, horn honks, and thumbs up he got from fellow motorists. They said truckers in particular would honk and nod almost reverently. My guess is they appreciate a good place to go on the road more than just about anyone.

As I had hoped, the outhouse was a beauty. First of all, and most importantly, it had a moon carved into the front door. To me this is as essential as a well-designed cup holder in your car: The rest is gravy. The inside featured a comfortable one-hole bench sanded silky smooth for comfort.

I went about painting and sealing. For the exterior, I chose a rich forest green; for the interior I used a clear latex wood sealer to preserve the natural woodgrain. For the critically important undercarriage underneath the bench, I slapped on coat after coat of the heaviest oil-based sealer money could buy.

The following week, my friends Paul and Jim showed up. Using plans provided in the manual by the Green Mountain Club, we went to work sawing and drilling pressure-treated six-by-sixes to build the cage where the outhouse would sit.

We had lengthy discussions as to exactly where the outhouse should be sited. This was no trivial decision, as we needed to factor in both environmental and aesthetic considerations, not to mention privacy and ease of access. So after a night around the campfire and a few cocktails, the moldering privy planning board (MPPB) came to its decision: We chose a flat spot in the upper woods—lower than the spring—and a short walk, but not too short, from the campfire; with good birding and a fine view of both the stream and the woods. We agreed it was a spot where one could leave the door open—both literally and figuratively—so he could, as Thoreau said, "live deliberately, to front only the essential facts of life," all while taking a nice, pleasant shit.

The next day, with the jobsite moved to the final location, we completed the cage. First, we installed two layers of heavy screening to keep duff and red wigglers in and blowflies and mice out. Mice, lovely creatures that they are, apparently like to line their nests with bits of used toilet paper. Gross again. Then we drove four-foot lengths of rebar through the six-by-sixes and into the ground to secure it from a tornado.

We dragged the outhouse up the hill with ropes and bolted it to the top of the cage with metal brackets. Then we attached a three-step stairway with a moss-covered rock doorstep rolled there by Jim. Last, I loaded a layer of duff, followed by the red wigglers I had been saving in a cooler.

It really did look lovely there hidden in the woods. Its deep-forest-green exterior blended perfectly with the surroundings. Mimi generally steers clear of the outhouse but did provide me with various accoutrements to make an outhouse an outhome. A vintage metal shelf from a barber shop holds toilet paper and hand sanitizer, and a wire rack of magazines serves as the library: the current *Farmer's Almanac*, a *National Lampoon* from 1973, an *Alaska Sportsman* from 1954, and a small book of classic fishing quotes. A pair of binoculars hangs from a hook in case something of note flies by or perches. An old porcelain sign is screwed to the door outside that says "Gents," but please know that all are welcome, regardless of gender.

So what does an outhouse tucked into a hillside in the Catskill Mountains have to do with trout fishing? Try this: It's a pleasant morning in May, and you follow the wooded trail leading to the privy. You have a seat and push open the door onto a landscape painting of hemlocks and ferns. An ovenbird's sharp call pierces the woods somewhere behind you. The stream rushes along at a perfect fishing level. Later you will make a quick pass through a few pools with the two-weight. Come afternoon, you will gear up and head for the big river to look for March browns. Maybe there will be a spinner fall this evening. The day reads like a menu in the finest restaurant. Right now, you can sit and consider them all, untroubled, knowing that your footsteps on this gentle land remain light.

June 22: Finn is sleepy, and who can blame him? We took a long, rambling hike in the woods. Then we walked in the stream, armed with nets, stalking, catching, and releasing various frogs, salamanders, and crayfish. Finally, we topped the day off with a quick swim, or at least a dunking, in one of the deeper pools. A big day for a soon-to-be second-grader. Now he can barely keep his eyes open.

The campfire pops loudly, startling him for a second, but his eyes quickly go back to drooping slits. A minute later, Mimi walks him inside. He can barely wish me good night and good luck. He'll be out cold in 10 minutes.

Time to gather my tackle.

By late June, with fewer hatches and warming water, trout fishing on the Delaware is concentrated to a 45-minute window at dusk. This means I can have a leisurely dinner and even dessert by the fire and not miss much of anything in terms of rising fish or hatches. But by 8:15, it's time to move.

I grab my vest, waders, and rod; toss them into the back of the car; and drive to the river.

The spot is private, a gift from friendships forged here over the last decade. I park and scramble down the steep bank. The sun has just dipped below the far mountain, leaving a halo of gold above it. Fifty feet above me, I can see the last shafts of direct sunlight glint off a few mayfly spinners—sulfurs probably. A good sign.

I sit on a rock and wait. I check my leader and apply floatant to the sulfur spinner knotted to the tippet. Overhead the silhouette of an eagle hurries downstream.

The river quiets. The few warblers still calling this late in the season have settled to roost. Even the veeries are down to their single "dwerp" call, meaning for them, too, it's nearly bedtime.

V-wakes of a few late-season shad slowly cut across the surface in front of me. Some will still rise to a fly, but I avoid casting to them. They are largely spent now, carrying half their body weight than when they swam into this pool two months ago. Time to let them be.

A few minutes later, the first trout rises midriver. Then a second fish joins it ten feet upstream. I remain seated on the rock, waiting for the light to further dim, cuing more mayfly spinners to hit the water, deposit their eggs, and die.

Both fish tilt up and feed again. The rises are unrushed and deliberate. Think of putting the first roll on your plate at the beginning of a very long buffet line. By the next set of rises, I stand up. It's nearly dark now, so my instinct to hunch over is probably overkill, though I do it anyway.

I decide on which fish to target. The upstream fish is closer to the bank, so I head upriver, creeping along the shoreline in and out of river shallows and tall grasses.

The trout I've chosen is now rising in a more-greedy rhythm. It comes up gently every 10 or 15 seconds. The buffet is clearly getting more interesting. I quietly make my way a few feet above it, then wade out into the river, moving a foot or two closer each time it rises.

I stop and strip line from the reel. Downstream, over the blackness of the mountain, the sky still shines silver, and I line up the reflection on the water so I can see the trout rising and my fly when it drops. Hopefully I will see the take, too.

I wait for the trout to come up again. When it does, I cast and try to follow the descending fly with my eyes to see where it lands. But I lose it in the darkness. The trout sips something off the surface, and I lift—into nothing. Swing and a miss.

A barred owl calls from upriver. The first stars have appeared. Behind me, Jupiter hangs low and bright.

I make another cast and again can't see where the fly lands. Either it's darker than I think, or my middle age eyes are, well, acting their age. Probably a little of both.

The trout rises again. I lift tentatively and am immediately rewarded with ponderous head shakes followed by a burst of drag from my reel that pierces the silence of the river. Of all the types of trout fishing I do, this may be the most satisfying. It is nothing short of hitting a homerun blindfolded.

The trout leaps somewhere out in the darkness, and the sound of it reentering the river echoes off the steep bank behind me. I back toward the shore, holding the rod high and winding line back onto the reel. I coax the trout closer and closer. Then I click on my headlamp to at least get a look. A lost fish without so much as a glimpse is the stuff of nightmares.

It swims into the light's beam, and I can see it is a long rainbow—better than 18 inches. Even if it gets off now. I will at least sleep tonight.

And then I've got the leader in one hand, and then the fish is cradled in the other. The fly is caught just in the scissor of its jaws, and I slip it free. Then I ease the trout into the current and watch it swim away, fading, and then gone.

I look at my watch: 9:20. There's still a fair amount of light left in the sky and maybe even another fish rising if I explored upstream or downstream a bit. But I made my point.

I hike up the steep bank and put the fly rod in the back of the car and shrug off my vest. Then I do something peculiar to this spot: I leave my waders on—a sort of reminder that I am six minutes from home and they can wait. Who cares if the seat is damp in the morning?

I drive back slowly, dodging toads that come out after dark, probably drawn to the heat still clinging to the road.

By the time I get back, Finn's asleep, and Mimi is on the porch, reading a book. I peel off my waders and hang them on the hook outside of the Walleye Room, then slip on my shoes. The night air feels cool against my clothes, which have dampened from sweat and condensation. I invite Mimi to join me at the fire pit. Then I put a log on the coals and blow a few times. They glow and smoke and then flame. Then they lap around the log, which begins to crackle and burn.

Mimi, anticipating a fishing story from me, has brought out a bottle and two metal camp cups. I hear the twist of a cork, then the splash of liquid. Robert Traver in Testament of a Fisherman *said, "bourbon out of an old tin cup always tastes better out there." And he is right.*

The 100-Years Mouse War and Other Skirmishes

My friend Dave once landed an extraordinarily fat 16-inch wild brown in a small, overlooked trout stream. It was a true blimp of a fish. He decided to take it home for dinner, as he liked to do once or twice a year. When he gutted it and opened its stomach, out plopped two partially digested mice.

So here's the joke I made up:

What do you call two dead mice in a trout's stomach?

A good start.

Mice. In the woods, they are admittedly adorable, with their long whiskers, big ears, and funny long tails. And ecologically speaking, they are a crucial cog in a well-functioning forest. Hawks and owls scarf them down by the talonful like a bowl of furry popcorn. Ditto for foxes, weasels, bobcats, and other rodent-loving predators. When they are not being eaten themselves, mice in turn eat pest insects and disperse seeds in their comings and goings. Yep, mice are so darned important.

But when they enter my cabin, they become one thing: a disgusting, pooping, peeing, gnawing, scratching, disease-carrying scourge with a bull's-eye between their beady little eyes. I wasn't always this ruthless.

I had a few early inklings that mice might be an issue at the cabin. I remember looking in the kitchen the day we bought the

place and noticing several metal storage lockers left behind. They were closed up tight like an abandoned fort in hostile country. What were they trying to keep out?

A few days later while doing some general clean-up outside, I decided to remove an abandoned phoebe nest above one of the windowsills. When I took it down, I noticed how it looked more like a mossy mound rather than the traditional cup shape of a bird's nest. Strange. I walked over to show it to Mimi, who considered it for a few seconds. Then she asked, "What's that hanging off the bottom?"

I flipped it over and saw a long tail sticking out from between sticks and moss. Then another tail unfurled. And another. Then it began to tremble and shake in my hands. I spastically flung the nest away from me. When it hit the ground, it disintegrated into five or six mice, which immediately bolted off in every direction. Three of them darted into various nooks underneath the cabin. Not long after that incident, I saw the back end of a dead mouse hanging out of a hole in an outside light fixture by the porch door. Apparently, it had gotten fatally wedged trying to find a way inside. When I pulled out its stiff little body by the tail, I could almost see a look of deranged determination on its face.

But other than those initial instances, we remained largely mouse-free for the first couple of seasons. I attribute this to a strict clean-up regimen at the end of each weekend. We were like the Grinch, leaving behind a crumb too small for a mouse. Actually, we didn't even leave that.

Then one spring, I loaned the cabin out to a couple of fishing buddies for the weekend. Unfortunately, they did not abide by our Grinch-crumb philosophy. The day they left, chasing a morning hatch of blue-winged olives on the Delaware, they hurriedly closed the place up but forgot their half-eaten breakfast on the porch. When I discovered it the next weekend, there were some mouse droppings on the plates, and napkins had been shredded into little pieces. My friends rightfully blamed the hatching mayflies.

Right after that we began to hear scurrying above us late at night. I'd wake up to the sound of tiny footsteps running back and forth in the ceiling and the crawl space. We jokingly called this "Mouse Olympics" and considered it more of a minor annoyance than anything. So far, except for the incident on the porch, we found no additional evidence that mice had ventured into the living space of the cabin. So, at least temporarily, we decided to cede the crawl space and ceiling. You could say an uneasy truce fell over the land. We were South Korea and North Korea. We were a tinderbox.

Shortly thereafter I discovered an apparent incursion into the demilitarized zone: a few mouse droppings in the bedroom on the floor at the foot of the wall. I swept them up, not sure if they had somehow fallen from a gap in the ceiling or were deposited on site. That night, all doubt was erased.

It was cold. Mimi, curled up under blankets in bed, fell asleep with the light on. She woke up at around midnight and sleepily reached beneath the lampshade to turn it off. But she didn't feel a light switch. She felt fur.

Mimi does not shriek by nature. This was more like a gasp of horror that sounded like "euuu-ahhh!" The mouse, looking almost indignant that someone interrupted its lightbulb sauna, shimmied down the lamp, hurried across the floor and vanished in the gap where the wall met the floor. Later, during what turned out to be a mostly sleepless night, we could hear Mouse Olympics raging above us.

The next day I drove into town and bought my first snap traps. Three seemed like it would take care of the problem (ha!). Then I got a ladder from the shed and, for the first time, opened the window in the crawl space. Up to this point, I had never even looked up there.

The window was on hinges but painted shut, so I first had to take a flathead screwdriver and a hammer and tap around the edges to break the seal. Then I pushed, and with a creak, the window swung inward. Out rushed thick, warm air. I clicked on a headlamp and peered inside. It looked like a typical crawl space: dark, close, and maybe a tad spooky. The first thing I noticed was an empty and ancient-looking box of rat poison lying in front of me, so this confirmed that these recent incursions were clearly not the debut for critters in the cabin. Then I noticed some mouse droppings scattered about, along with various dead insects—mostly moths and a few ants. Where the roofline met the floor of the crawl space, I could see what looked like softball-sized clumps of leaves—clearly mouse nests.

I stayed outside the entire time, feet firmly planted on the ladder. I had no intention of crawling into this house of horrors. Guys Who Fix Stuff may have shimmied right on in and, with a Shop Vac, sucked up the nests with one hand while maybe checking out the wiring with the other. But not this guy (I'm pointing at myself). Plus, I was worried I might crash through the ceiling and land in the Dairy Queen sink below.

But I did set the three snap traps, baiting each with a smear of peanut butter. Then I closed the window, put the ladder away, grabbed the two-weight, and went trout fishing. We drove back to New Jersey later that day.

The next weekend, we opened the cabin and walked into a faint, sickly sweet odor of decay. I immediately got the ladder, strapped on the headlamp, and looked in the crawl space. All three traps scored clean kills. I tossed the dead mice into the woods, opened some windows to air the place out, and rewarded myself with more fishing. Problem solved.

Ummm, no.

In cabin lore, it will always be known as: "The Night the Bedroom Became Known as 'The Mouse Room.'" Mimi unfortunately once again starred in this drama. At 2:00 a.m., something woke her from a deep sleep. She opened her eyes and lay there for a few seconds. It was quiet as a tomb. Then she felt it: a barely perceptible—but definite—tugging coming from her hair. Eyes now like saucers, she was petrified, unable to move, hoping, praying it would stop. But it didn't. A few seconds later she couldn't take it anymore. She shot upright, turned on the light, and looked wildly around. But there was nothing there. She rubbed her hair where she thought she had felt the tugging. Maybe it was a dream.

As to what happened next, I've come to imagine the famous horse head scene in *The Godfather*. Mimi slowly turned and looked at her pillow. And there it was—no, not a mouse; instead a calling card: a single turd left behind like a devilish mint.

I was awoken by a loud "euuu-ahhh!"

The next day, I bought a dozen more traps. I set them in the kitchen, bedroom, and crawl space, and if Mimi had let me, I would have set one on her pillow. But the weekend was over, and so once again, we had to return to New Jersey but this time with the cabin booby-trapped like a Vietcong bunker.

During the week, I learned more about our opponent. From pictures I found online, I recognized it as a white-footed mouse. Think of it as the more countrified version of your regulation New York City house mouse. But these were no bumpkins; like their urbanized counterparts, they could inflict serious damage to your home, such as gnawing through solid walls and chewing through electric wiring like it was overcooked spaghetti. They retained the usual repertoire of mouse unpleasantries, such as pooping 50 times a day (imagine!) and scent-marking by pissing pretty much constantly. An added bonus was the Lyme disease connection—white-footed mice serve as the main vector for deer ticks to spread Lyme to humans. On top of all this, I learned that they could fit into an opening the size of a dime by essentially detaching and reattaching parts of their skeletons. Their main defense against predators—or humans—is simple reproduction. They are capable of producing up to four litters of six young a year, and their off-spring become sexually mature at a scant two months. The more I read, the more I felt like I was facing some sort of slobbish, dis-eased, comic-book supervillain—and a randy one at that.

The next weekend, we again walked into the smelly after-math of battle. A dead mouse lay in the kitchen, and I found two more felled in the crawl space. Once again, we cleaned up and aired out. But later that day, they retaliated, when Mimi opened a drawer of my fly-tying desk on the porch and stared down at a platoon of reinforcements: six pinkish babies squirming in the center of a nest made from the feathers of one of my best dry-fly rooster capes. I was in the other room when I heard the now telltale "euuu-ahhh!" When I ran onto the porch, Mimi had already slammed the drawer shut. She stood there, pointing with one hand and covering her mouth with the other. I wrenched the drawer from the desk, ran outside, and flung it as far as I could, sending feathers and baby mice flying. Clearly, I had lost myself in the savagery of battle. I stood there for a minute or so taking deep breaths, trying to calm myself by imagining I was releasing a brookie from the six-foot-wide stream, which still gurgled along carefree just a few yards away.

Later, I climbed underneath the cabin to see if I could find out how mice were getting inside and plug up any potential entryways. I stuffed gobs of steel wool in seemingly miniscule gaps where pipes led into the cabin. But as I lay there looking around, I could see that there were infinite openings: around floor joists, where piers met the bottom framing, and then outside, where each of the rough-cut boards overlapped each other. Most would have failed the dime test. The only way to truly keep mice out would be to enshroud the entire cabin in quarter-inch steel-mesh screening. And believe me, at that point, I considered it.

But then I learned about the bucket trap. My neighbor and sometimes fishing companion Mark, who owns a cottage down the road, told me about it and in fact loaned me a prototype he had recently made. Here's how it works: You take an empty spackle bucket and cut two opposing notches along the rim. Then you take a metal coffee can and drill a hole in the bottom and through the lid and run a thin rope through it. You fit the rope in each of the opposing notches in the bucket and knot it tightly so that the can suspends over it and it can spin freely. Then you bait the outside of the coffee can with a smear of peanut butter on each side so it acts like a counterbalance. Lastly you fill the bucket with about six inches of water and set a little wooden ramp that leads up to the lip (any piece of scrap wood will do). The mouse smells the peanut butter, runs up the ramp, and then jumps on the can, which rolls like a lumberjack log. And then—well, it drowns.

OK, some of you may be thinking that this is cruel, drowning poor little mice. Two things: First, I understand from the Internet that drowning may actually be one of the more pleasant ways to expire. Second, get back to me after your wife had a mouse shit on her pillow.

The bucket trap turned into a veritable mouse vacuum. It sucked up entire mouse families. I scored doubles, triples, even quintuples on some nights. Apparently, mice don't care if their compatriots drown when peanut butter is involved.

Eventually my hauls dwindled and then tapered into nothing. The battle, finally, had ended, but I know the war never will.

Maybe once a season, I hear scurrying above us, and when I do, I unleash the bucket trap in the crawl space. I've since built my own, and it's a beauty—a real killer. The morning after, I simply take the bucket and dump its contents into the stream and watch the victims drift away. Presumably the corpses sink to the bottom and make a few crayfish very happy. Or maybe one or two drift all the way to the Delaware, where an enormous brown gleefully gulps them down, adding to the good start begun by Dave's fish long ago.

Right about the time the mouse wars subsided, a new pest slithered onto the property. I began seeing a few here and there in early June, and then suddenly they exploded in numbers that could only be described as biblical—in that nasty Old Testament sort of way. Yes, I was experiencing my first eruption of forest tent caterpillars.

Tim simply called them "worms." There were thousands; make that tens of thousands; no, make that millions; no make that . . . you get the point. They were about two inches long, blackish, and covered in bristly hair, with a white keyhole pattern running up their soft, mushy backs. They crawled across the grass, dangled from strands of silk like rappelling mountaineers, and of course ate trees—lots and lots of trees. I first noticed something was not right when, on the ride up, I drove through several stands of woods that should have been dark with shade and lushly leafed out. Instead they looked like the stark forests of November. The caterpillars had stripped them bare.

When we pulled into the driveway and got out of the car, I heard what sounded like light rain. Except it was sunny. No, it was not the sound of nibbling leaves. It was caterpillar frass gently pitter-pattering through the canopy and onto the ground. While frass might sound like a condiment offered at a Starbucks ("More frass on your grande macchiato?") it is actually just a really nice word for caterpillar shit. It resembled freshly ground black pepper and covered virtually everything.

By the way, "forest tent caterpillar" is a misnomer—these repugnant insects are not the same ones that build the tents you sometimes see in trees along highways. Instead, they wander the woods until they find a tree—preferably a sugar maple, birch, ash, beech, or a few other hardwoods. And then they lay waste to it, defoliating it in a matter of days. In case you forgot, the hardwoods on the property are mostly sugar maple, birch, ash, and beech. Most trees can survive one defoliation, maybe even a second, but it can weaken already-stressed trees so that other diseases can administer a final coup de grâce. How many of my trees were already stressed due to the recent floods? I decided I would not stand idly by and find out. And so, as the Clash wrote in the song "London Calling," war is declared, and battle come down.

My first efforts were downright silly. I squashed caterpillars whenever I saw them, or I just tossed them into the stream. The latter tactic proved to be particularly futile, as I found out that the caterpillar's many hairs served as its own personal floatation device. They would simply bob and drift to the nearest backwater until they reached a streamside rock. Then they would climb ashore, drip dry, and eat more trees.

But then I remembered from grammar school science class that you could break the surface tension of water by adding soap to it. So I filled a bucket with stream water and squeezed in a few drops of dishwasher detergent. Then I dropped in a caterpillar. It sank like a rock—a hairy, disgusting one. So for the rest of the day, I drowned caterpillars by the gross, gathering squirming handfuls and depositing them in the bucket. At the end of the weekend, I poured the whole mess out in the woods and let the burying beetles and flies take care of the rest. Still, I knew this was futile—like trying to bail out the ocean with a sippy cup.

Back home in New Jersey, hard at work at my new job of researching vermin attacking the cabin, I learned that forest tent caterpillars are social critters. At night they tend to come down from the trees they have spent the day eating and gather by the hundreds around the trunk for some R&R. Come morning, they slither back up and continue denuding.

This gave me an idea. The next Saturday morning at the cabin, I woke up early armed with two rolls of duct tape and something called Tree Tanglefoot—a super-sticky goo made from tree sap. You applied it with a caulk gun, and it acted as a natural barrier to keep nonflying critters from climbing up trees and shrubs. Knowing there was no way to protect all 14 acres, I chose about 20 of my favorite hardwoods around the cabin and along the stream. I convinced myself that, if I could safeguard them, then at least I could sleep at night. So I took the duct tape and wrapped each tree. This would serve as the base to apply the goo. Then I circled each tree, squirting a continuous bead on the duct tape. Lastly, I took an old paint scraper and used it to spread the stuff, which was thicker than molasses. It was a sticky, awful job. No matter how much I tried to protect myself with rubber gloves, I wound up getting gooey glop all over my hands, face, and clothes.

But, by God, it worked. The caterpillars couldn't cross the barriers I created. Those that attempted got stuck and died. The rest gathered by the hundreds around this Maginot Line of stickiness. You could almost see their little caterpillar brains stuck in a sort of endless loop: "Sticky. Bad. Sticky. Bad. Sticky. Bad."

With thousands of juicy caterpillars now waylaid around the base of 20 trees, I thought the local bird population would have gorged on such an easy food source, but apparently, only the black-billed cuckoo eats forest tent caterpillars in any numbers. Cuckoos have an adaptation that allows them to deal with those nasty bristly hairs by coughing up a sort of hairball when they're full. Unfortunately, only a few cuckoos pass through each spring. I would have needed a Hitchcockian-sized flock to make a dent in the population.

I sat on the porch and lamented. The gentle hiss of the stream now intermingled with the sound of falling frass. If only there was something else that would eat the caterpillars.

There was. Flies. Or more specifically, maggots.

Just as the caterpillars began to cocoon, plagues of several species of parasitic flies descended. Some laid eggs on the caterpillars themselves; others would deposit a live—and hungry—maggot on the cocoon. Either way, the caterpillar or pupal moth soon became dinner—or lunch or breakfast.

The most prolific of these is nicknamed the "friendly fly"—because, when they are not laying eggs on caterpillar cocoons, they simply adore landing on your arms, legs, face, or any part of your exposed skin to rest or perhaps lap up some salt. They don't bite, but they are beyond annoying. If you sat outside for more than 30 seconds, three would immediately fly over to say howdy. Wait another 30 seconds, and another three would join the party, et cetera. Shoo them away, and they would aloft, circle around, and land again. I suppose if you didn't move at all, you may have eventually resembled one of those Ripley's Believe It or Not guys with the bee beards. Thus, the next two weekends were hellish. Between the flies and caterpillars, it made me long for the halcyon days of slinging baby mice across the yard.

If there was one benefit to all of this—and only one—I discovered that trout in the six-foot-wide stream loved to eat forest tent caterpillar moths. The caterpillars themselves they largely ignored, but the tannish, delta-winged moths they truly relished. Each night, I would gather a dozen or two in less than 30 seconds around my porch light and keep them in a jar until morning. Then I would shake the jar, stunning them just enough so they couldn't fly. Then I'd sprinkle them on the stream. The resulting fireworks show was impressive, with brookies and rainbows flinging themselves from the water with glee, taking down moth after moth until they had eaten every last one.

By July, it was all over. My backyard felt like the aftermath of some dystopian battlefield. Bits of chewed leaves lay scattered about; duct tape laden with dead caterpillars draped from trees, empty cocoons—some parasitized, others hatched—dotted trees and overhangs along the cabin. Thankfully, virtually all of my hardwoods survived. Even the ones that I couldn't protect grew a second, albeit smaller, set of leaves.

I was in the middle of peeling one of the duct tape traps from a tree when Tim came walking down the driveway. He saw what I was doing and said, "Hope it's not as bad next year. Usually lasts three years."

Like when I first learned about fracking, I sputtered, "Wait—what?"

And he was right; for the next two seasons, come June, I was back to taping trees with sticky glop and brushing off squadrons of friendly flies who wanted to be my best buddy.

I had a front-row seat of a great arms race between the caterpillars and flies, with the flies eventually gaining the upper hand and tamping down the caterpillar population to near nothing by year four. But with no food, the fly population must inevitably crash, which will allow the caterpillars to eventually come slithering back. They haven't yet, but when they do, I'll be ready to welcome them with a particularly boisterous "euuuu-ahhhh!"

July 6: Picture the six-foot-wide stream with the same rushing and tumbling character, but make it 10 times wider and give it 20 times the volume. Then cover the bottom with uneven, superslick boulders and cobble that make wading feel more like mountaineering. Then populate it with a decent crop of wild brookies and browns and make a few of them large. That's the place.

I only wish it was closer. But it's an hour from the cabin, so it is now down to a once- or twice-a-season pilgrimage. Before we bought our place, I would visit it almost weekly when it fished well. The one good part is that, when most closer streams are well past their seasonal peak, this one is just hitting its stride, thanks to cold water and a healthy population of late-hatching stoneflies.

It's muggy when I pull into the turn-off, so I decide to wet-wade in quick-dry pants and wading sandals with nonslip soles. A folding wading staff holstered to my belt along with my vest, and I am all set. I hike upstream along a lightly used trail to my favorite stretch—a quarter-mile of pockets, sluices, and bubbly runs. When I step in, the water feels cold but not numbingly so—I would say mid-60s, perfect for risers. Then I check one of the many protruding boulders for stonefly husks. There are at least a dozen, flattened and with a white zipper mark along their heads where the adult crawled out of its shell. I survey other rocks and see dozens more.

I tie on a size 10 Stimulator—the same fly I might use for the six-foot-wide stream. But here, it is rigged to a carefully constructed nine-foot 4x leader strung to a limber eight-foot five-weight rod. And here I will actually try to land the fish—not just count the number of times something comes up, swipes, and misses.

The first spot is one of the few true pools along this stretch. A strong head of water rushes in at the top, briefly slows around a single large boulder, and then organizes and hurries into the next riffle. Nothing lingers in this fast, narrow river. I stand knee deep, and with the sound of rapids above and below, I strip off 30 feet of line and make a cast. The Stimulator shoots across the pool and lands in the bubble line at the far side of the boulder. I know what's about to happen. And it does. A trout comes up for the fly, and I miss it. And then it doesn't come back. The same game is played out nearly every time I cast to this one spot. I always bite; the fish rarely does.

I move up to the next run, and the water is now thigh deep. A little more bracing, but better than waders on this 80-degree humid day. Here a slightly deeper slot maybe two feet wide and six feet long causes the water to slow just enough to attract a trout. It's a subtle holding lie; the first two years I fished here, I waded right past it. But then one day I decided to make a cast, and as Robert Frost said, that has made all the difference.

The fly lands. I hold the rod out and upward, keeping line and leader off the water. It bobs along among a trail of bubbles. A sleek brown trout cruises upward, takes, and hurries back to the bottom with the fly in its mouth. I set the hook, and the fish darts and jabs. But in a minute or so, it's in my hand: a 12-incher. Tannish, with relatively few spots but some of them distinctly red. I admire the brown for a few more seconds, then open my fingers. It shoots away.

I continue wet-wading through the stretch. A shaded pocket on the far bank gives up a ten-inch brookie. I miss a violent strike where two tongues of current briefly convene. Though I cast several more times, there is no repeat showing. Here, more so than on other streams I know, fish hardly ever come back for a second look.

After a while, I take a break and sprawl out on a large flat river rock warmed by the sun. It feels good on wet, chilled legs. I chew down a granola bar and chase it with a few gulps of water. Slipping and sliding and fighting the current takes its toll. From upriver, a mottled immature bald eagle flies low down the corridor, looking particularly immense in these relatively narrow confines. I watch it pass as it continues downstream and around the next bend.

Break time is over, and I slide back into the river. I wade through rapids using my wading staff to reach a particular run just above them. Here, on the far side of the river, a series of wheelbarrow-sized boulders direct the current into a sort of long trough. For some reason, this spot nearly always holds a decent brook trout. And again, it does not disappoint. The fish takes with a confident gulp and after zipping around the run and nearly between my legs comes to my hand. It is a large female, a foot long, dark from the tannin-stained water, and deep-bodied presumably from gorging on stoneflies.

I fight the current some more, shooting cast after cast to likely spots. Like on the six-foot-wide stream, the scattergun approach pays off. Two smaller browns come from unlikely looking pockets, and I raise and miss another fish just at the tail of a larger pool.

All the while, I have been saving my favorite spot for last. It's only the size of a Jacuzzi but belt-buckle deep. A small waterfall drops in from between two boulders, and a sluice of current sneaks in from the side. Again, I need to battle through rapids to reach it. By now, a couple of hours of immersion have left my legs feeling less than limber.

I reach my knee-deep perch and take a minute to stretch my back while surveying the best location to place a fly. I decide to bounce it off the boulder at the head of the pool to see if something is resting in the eddy to the side of the waterfall. But two casts there, and nothing takes. On the third one, I let the fly drift longer. When the current takes it below me, I lift the rod and twitch it once. Then twice. A trout shoots up, flashing gold, and takes the fly down. It greyhounds wildly over the pool, then tries to power under the big boulder at the head. I check the rod low and, with the current on my side, force the trout to change its mind. It does, shooting past me and exiting the pool. I stand my ground and let the fish fight itself out as it tries to make its way under this boulder and then that one. It eventually tires and winds up in the eddy formed below my legs. I rest the rod under one arm and slip a hand underneath a heavy 15-inch brown. With the other hand, I twist the fly free. The fish rests for another second, finning below my legs. Then, as if it realized for the first time it is a foot away from me, it bolts across the current and back into the Jacuzzi-sized pool.

Back at the car, I break down the rod and shed my vest and, with no one around, quickly change into dry shorts. I gulp down the rest of the water. These last few hours will definitely be felt tomorrow. I drive back to the cabin with the windows up for a while, the hot car feeling good on my thawing legs.

The Bird Hatch

Each spring, I know we have not opened the cabin too early when I pull into the driveway, open the car door, and immediately hear a phoebe singing. They are among the first seasonal migrants, somber-colored in shades of gray matching the early spring woods. But they are members of the flycatcher family, which means bugs have started hatching from the six-foot-wide stream—probably early brown stoneflies but maybe some blue quills.

Their song is a wheezy, phonetic version of their name, usually repeated over and over: "*Phoe-be! Phoe-be!*" To me it sounds like they are having a sneezing fit. If we are lucky, a pair has already started to build a nest on the side of the cabin. These mud-and-grass structures are engineering marvels bordering on a magic trick; all the birds need is the smallest ledge or overhang for purchase to construct a moss-lined cup that hangs precariously over the ground. Depending on your perspective, the one drawback to having your cabin chosen by phoebes is that they are among the very first birds to begin singing each morning. Hearing "*Phoe-be!*" repeated 100 times at 5:00 a.m. is either soothing or nerve-racking. I'm in the former camp, but I've heard mixed reviews from some overnight guests.

I've often wondered why more trout anglers, particularly fly fishers, are not birders. You would think that their incessant need to identify aquatic insects, often down to their Latin names and sometimes by counting body segmentation or some other

anatomical doodad, would translate to a natural progression toward also wanting to know what's calling or flying around them along the stream. Sure, everyone ogles at a bald eagle as it soars past—who wouldn't? But give me an angler whose fishing report includes the sighting of a prothonotary warbler and I'm suitably impressed (plus I want to know where the hell he saw the bird).

The intricate songs of birds, some beautiful and haunting, some strange, and some downright goofy, are nothing less than the musical score of a trout stream and the surrounding woods. Without them, something essential is missing. Imagine the movie *The Last of the Mohicans* without its incredibly powerful overture—perhaps the greatest composition one can play (loudly, please) while imaging the mountains and forests of the Northeast. Without it, the movie would be just some corny flick with Daniel Day-Lewis running around with his shirt open.

My ace birding friends—many of whom are fine anglers, too—have identified around 100 species either around or near the 14 acres that make up my property. Some are less common than others, but none are particularly rare. They explain that this is what happens when you mix many acres of unbroken woods with a few farms and then throw in some streams and a larger river or two. The birds will do the rest.

I am not one of the ace birders. However, I am very good at sticking close to them and making sure I see everything they see and then ask a lot of questions. This is how I learned, for example, that the song of the yellow warbler, which sounds like *"Sweet, sweet, sweet, I'm so sweet"* is not the same as the chestnut-sided warbler's *"Pleased, pleased, pleased to meet you."* It's sort of like glomming onto a very good fisherman and along the way learning a secret leader formula or even a pet spot just because you asked to come along. To be unabashed is to be rewarded.

I consider myself extremely fortunate that the birders I learned from were not the tweedy types who might say, "Why that merlin is spec-*ta*-cular." Instead they argued and swore at each other—always in a good-natured way—over bird songs. Their phonetic interpretations were creative. Instead of such standards as *"old Sam Peabody"* for the white-throated sparrow or *"drink-your-teeeeee"* for a towhee, they made up their own, like for the white-eyed vireo, whose song—they say—is clearly *"Dick Vermeil shit!"* And they noted that the American redstart often ended its song with an emphatic *"aw fuck it."* Once, when a broad-winged hawk soared past, they all looked up through binoculars and watched it ride a thermal along a ridge. It would tack into the wind, then adjust its tail like a rudder to quickly turn the way a surfer would on a cresting wave. It seemed like a good 30 seconds went by, when one of them finally said, "Now there's a bird that's really got its shit together." The rest nodded reverently.

I have tried to watch birds with that same lens for approaching 30 years. I've never taken it so seriously that I maintain a "life list" like some birders do. Nor do I give a hoot about entire categories of hard-to-identify birds, like fall warblers, all of which look virtually the same. It's kind of like streamer fishing for trout in the early season. Some guys swear by it, but if I have to work that hard to hook a big fish, I'll pick up my spinning rod and cast for shad.

So with the authority of enthusiasm—but nothing more—I give you my completely random list of assorted birds of note around the cabin and the six-foot-wide stream. I start with other early migrants that follow the phoebe. Sometime in late April or early May, I hear a red-eyed vireo start to sing around the cabin— and it literally doesn't shut up until late July or sometimes later. Its phonetic "*here I am; over here*" goes on like the ranting of a crazy person, usually long after most other birds have not only stopped singing for the year but also have already begun to head south for the winter. It's nondescript-looking—kind of a tannish-gray— and if it has a red eye, I've never been close enough to see it first-hand. But what it lacks in rakish looks, it makes up in sheer vocal persistency. It is the constant companion of the cabin, and I'm glad it is over here, as it likes to remind me a thousand times a day.

The arrival of the vireo often coincides with the first Louisiana waterthrush. If there is one bird bonded with the six-foot-wide stream, it is this oddly named warbler. Occasionally I spot one along the streambanks, always mechanically bobbing its tail up and down as it hunts and pecks for insects. Not that I need a reminder, but its sharp-noted song at random times during the day reassures me that, yes, there is a native trout stream flowing past. One year, a pair built a teacup-sized nest in a beech tree just a few feet off the porch, and you could watch their comings and goings. The nest looked to be an intricate weaving of dried grasses, pieces of birch bark, and moss. Three tiny mottled eggs sat nestled in the center, cushioned and insulated by spiderwebbing gathered by either mom or dad. But then the 700-year flood of '06 came, and the associated cataclysm that went with it: the stream-cum-Niagara-River, the hundreds of doomed trees washing past, and of course the 15 inches of rain that instigated it all. Two weeks later, I sat on the porch with Mimi shell-shocked by the shambles of the stream when something flitted past. One of the waterthrushes swooped into the still-standing beech tree and fed its three hatched chicks as if nothing had happened. Because of that one moment, they will always remain among my favorites. After the chicks fledged, we carefully took down the nest, and it sits in a glass case back at home.

I vote veeries and hermit thrushes as the birds most likely to make me weep. Their incredibly sad songs, heard just before darkness sets in, often intertwine and seem to mourn the loss of each day. Think of it as "Taps" of the bird world. Yet I associate both of them with the joys of mayfly hatches and rising trout. Nature can be complicated.

Saying the scarlet tanager is pretty is like saying springtime is kind of nice. But as stunningly beautiful as they are, their singing ability is not only overlooked but also actually mocked by some birders, who describe it as a "raspy robin" or "robin with a sore throat." F. Schuyler Matthews disagrees. In *Field Book of Wild Birds and Their Music* (1904), he wrote of the tanager's song,

> *There is a lazy, drowsy, dozy buzz to this beautiful bird's voice which one can often liken to a giant musical bumblebee, or an old-time hurdy-gurdy; the unobtrusive music speaks of summer's peace and rest, soft zephyrs blowing over sighing pine trees, and tinkling shallows of woodland brooks.*

Amen, Schuyler. The tanager's domain is normally high in the canopy, offering only a glimpse of their electric-red plumage as they flit from branch to branch. But one time at the cabin, a male literally tried to run me off the place. It was an unusually cold May afternoon, and I went for a quick hike up the dirt road that follows the stream. Something bright red caught my eye low in a branch just off the road. A tanager. As I went for my binoculars, the bird took off, flew straight at me, and then veered off ten feet from my head like a strafing Messerschmitt. I looked around confused, then realized I was wearing my red-

and-black-checked wool coat. I must have looked like the condor of tanagers. Brave bird.

Two other warblers, the black-throated green and blackburnian, nest somewhere in the hemlocks behind the cabin and, like the vireo, are vocal companions through most of May and June (though they seem to at least take coffee breaks and siestas). Both birds are lookers—particularly the blackburnian, with its orange head streaked in black. It amazes me that both species, not much longer than the average brookie in the stream and each weighing less than an ounce, make determined migrations to the tropics and even farther (the blackburnian winters in the Andes). Then they return again the next spring, using the sun, stars, and the earth's electromagnetic fields as their GPS.

My Kauffman *Field Guide to Birds of North America* accurately describes the winter wren as a "stub-tailed gnome . . . creeping like a rodent under fallen logs, through dense thickets and along streambanks." It also sounds like it has a triple espresso each morning. Its song is a rapid-fire diatribe of melodic notes on speed and maybe hallucinogens. I've seen one just once—picture a brown ping-pong ball with a bill and stubby tail rolling along willy-nilly through the undergrowth. One time, Paul and Jim, both excellent birders, were midargument over some sort of warbler call when a winter wren erupted in song nearby. Jim kept talking to make his point, but Paul stopped immediately. When the wren had finished his song, Paul turned to Jim and said, "Don't *ever* interrupt a winter wren." And Jim hasn't since. None of us have. The winter wren always has the floor.

I am not a bird hunter, but there are gamebirds here, including wild turkey, woodcock, and a single beat-up pheasant I once saw in the driveway that looked like an escaped stocked bird. But my favorite is the ruffed grouse. The drumming of the male—a sound made purely by beating its wings, sometimes by standing on a hollow stump that it uses as an amplifier—sounds like an old lawnmower sputtering, then coming to life. It drums usually early in the morning for an hour or so and has occasionally brightened a trip to the moldering privy. Once or twice each fall, I spook one in the woods—or rather it spooks me, exploding from the forest floor with booming wings. As I said, I do not hunt, but each time one flies off zig-zagging between trees, my inner caveman tells me I should be reaching for my atlatl.

For raptors, we have ho-hum bald eagles pretty much all over the big river, particularly after shad finish spawning and swim lazily along the surface with a large bull's-eye on their scales. Various hawks soar around, too, and occasionally hunt in the woods behind the cabin. The local songbird population always seems to tip off their whereabouts. Pleasant songs suddenly turn to sharp and raspy alarm calls, and then a red-shouldered hawk comes skulking out of a spruce tree, as if saying "OK, OK, you caught me." But my favorite bird of prey around here is the barred owl, which, despite their reputation as strictly nocturnal, will sometimes decide to call at 12:00 noon. Even so, my favorite time to hear them is while reeling up my fly line at 9:30 in the evening after the trout have finally stopped rising on the big river—the feathered version of the fat lady singing. It occurred to me that, as many times as I've heard barred owls, I've never actually seen one at the cabin. This is true with many birds; I hear far more than actually see. The songs are good enough. It's like the trout in the stream. I don't have to catch every one to appreciate them.

Then there is the wackiest bird of all: the yellow-bellied sapsucker, which nonbirding friends always think is a made-up species. It is very real. During the spring, the males fly from tree to tree, knocking out a rhythmic call that has almost a Latin flair: "Bang-ba-bang-bang! Bang-bang-bang!" But they don't just hammer on trees. For instance, the metal gutter hanging from the porch seems to have pleasing acoustics. One Friday in late spring, we pulled up at around 7:30 in the evening. As we began to unpack, I heard a loud, metallic "Bang-ba-bang-bang!

Bang-bang-bang!" coming from the porch, I peered around just in time to see a yellow-bellied sapsucker fly from the gutter. As we hurried luggage and food into the cabin, I heard it three more times. I realized it had found a new favorite sounding board, and I wondered if it would continue its call in the morning.

At 6:02 a.m. my question was answered, when five feet from my sleeping head, "Bang-ba-bang-bang! Bang-bang-bang!"

"What the fu—?"

"Bang-ba-bang-bang! Bang-bang-bang!"

"Bang-ba-bang-bang! Bang-bang-bang!"

I shot up from the futon and ran outside in my underwear.

"Go away!"

The sapsucker casually flew across the stream and landed vertically on a yellow birch, giving me a sideways look.

I went back inside, got back under the blankets, and was just drifting back to sleep, when—

"Bang-ba-bang-bang! Bang-bang-bang!"

And so it went for the next hour: me running outside in my underwear and the sapsucker flying off but returning every three minutes to play on its new favorite snare drum. When it finally stopped, it did so not because of me. The only benefit from the incident was getting to tell Finn the story later that morning over breakfast. He was sleeping in the bedroom and never heard a thing. He laughed so hard, milk came out of his nose.

Then there are the birds that eat trout in the stream: namely great blue herons, kingfishers, and the dreaded common merganser, one of which single-handedly ate a dozen trout from the culvert pool, cleaning it out for the remainder of the season. I personally have nothing against these birds—they have to earn a living, too. I just wish they would either do it somewhere else or that a bear, bobcat, great horned owl, or take-your-pick predator would eat them.

I'm still learning new birds. A few weeks ago, I heard an unfamiliar bird singing above the stream. Its song was harsh and unrelenting, a raspy "*Che-beck, che-beck, che-beck, che-beck.*" So I got my binoculars, field guide, and iPod downloaded with various bird songs. I spotted it perched on a dead limb over the stream and watched it for a few seconds. Phoebe-like but smaller. It darted out and caught a bug, then returned to its perch and ate its catch. Definitely some sort of flycatcher, both in appearance and habit. After some cross-checking in the bird book and sampling a few calls, I positively identified it as a least flycatcher, a common species in the East frequently found along forest edges, according to the field guide. The right bird in the right place—just as it should be.

I since have learned that the least flycatcher has declined by an estimated 50 percent in much of its range. Unfortunately, many of the species mentioned—particularly the migratory warblers, tanagers, and vireos—all face precarious times. Grouse, too. Things like habitat loss, forest fragmentation from development, climate change, migratory obstacles, and domestic cats—which kill literally billions of birds a year—all take a toll. More death by a thousand cuts.

Like the trees that anchor the banks and shade the stream, the birds, too, are an essential part of this landscape. And not just because they look pretty and have interesting songs. They indirectly prevent erosion and keep streams shaded by dropping seeds along the banks and flood plains, they eat bugs that would otherwise strip certain trees bare, and they attract and galvanize people who are determined to protect wild nature. Lose the birds, and I fear the fish aren't far behind.

August 12: The birds have gone quiet, except for the ever-loquacious red-eyed vireo. But even its song sounds less emphatic, ebbing as the soft winds of late summer begin to blow themselves out. Earlier today, Tim mentioned he heard a hermit thrush this morning—a welcome song in the silence that is the August woods.

With windows down, I bounce along a dead-end dirt road with fallow farm fields on both sides. An abandoned barn, its roofline sagging like an ancient horse put out to pasture, nears collapse. Tim's family owns much of the land here—100 acres of former farms and woodlots. A stream runs through it, and in this stream a single pool awaits. I fish it just once a year, usually when the Delaware and six-foot-wide stream have hit their August slump.

I park where the road ends. In front of me, a clapboard farmhouse, roof gone, slowly turns to compost. Tim once told me his grandparents spent their first year as a married couple there some 70 years ago. I grab the two-weight, and with a small fly box and nippers shoved in the pocket of my shorts, I make my way down a former town road, now just a rugged trail.

The sound of the stream gradually comes in on the right. Before long, I see it 80 feet or so below me, paralleling the old road. One time I clambered down there and fished that stretch but found it to be mostly shallow flats with trout too widely spread out to make it worthwhile.

The grade steepens, and I traverse a few washouts. Tim said one of the big floods in the 1940s washed most of the road away, so the town took it off the books. Indeed, the stream seems eager to rise up and overtake it. But just before it gets its chance, I see—and hear—where it drops over a cliff and out of sight.

Below that is the pool I savor.

From the trail, 40 feet up, it certainly looks inviting: maybe 25 feet wide, round, and nearly waist-deep, which for this diminutive brook might as well be the Marianas Trench.

Here's another fact from Tim: In the late 1800s, a robbery took place in one of the long-gone farmhouses. Two thieves made their getaway on a horse and wagon, tearing down the road in the middle of the night. But they failed to negotiate a turn and plunged over the waterfall into the rocky pool below. Both were killed. No other trout pool I have ever fished comes with such legend and provenance.

The washed-out road ambles away into the woods. I veer off down a steep trail that will lead me to the pool. When I reach the bottom,

I can look upstream and for the first time behold the waterfall in its full splendor.

It is straight out of the Hudson River school—the dark, mossy greens of its rock face are framed by hemlocks on either side. A brushstroke of white, foaming water pinches through a narrow chasm, then widens, before plunging into the pool. I stand and watch it from afar for a few moments, feeling almost humbled that I can freely enter such a sacred landscape.

The stream runs slightly lower than normal, so I approach the pool cautiously, keeping low and stepping into it heron-like. The water feels precisely one degree warmer than ankle-aching.

I strip off line while false casting and then drop the fly—a Royal Wulff—to the right of the main tongue of current flowing from where the waterfall hits the pool. I already know what lives here and what I will soon behold: fine art in the form of two or three seven-inch brook trout, natives with red spotting so fine it seems like each one is individually and lovingly hand-painted.

But surprisingly, after several casts, no fish rise. So I lengthen my line and put the fly inches from the waterfall. It lands in a confusion of bubbles and current, then begins drifting quickly over the deepest part of the pool. A shaft of sunlight catches the white of the calf-tail wing just as a huge brook trout slashes and misses.

OH MY GOD, WHAT A TROUT!

The instant replay in my brain repeats these highlights: wide, salmon-colored pectoral fins flashing; water throwing; the violence of the rise heard over the rush of the waterfall.

My inner monologue kicks in, adapting a scene from Jaws, *a movie I've watched easily 100 times: "That's a 12-incher!" Hooper cries out.*

"Thirteen," Quint coolly counters. "Three-quarters of a pound of him."

A 13-inch brookie in this stream would be the same as a 60-pound striped bass in the surf. In a word, immense. I eagerly cast again. And again. And yet again. But the brookie resists.

I am shocked. Nearly every trout I've ever caught in this pool were beyond gullible, rising repeatedly until they practically impaled themselves on my hook.

But not this fish. I have found a cautious brook trout, and it's a large one. And I love it for that.

I look into my fly box and switch to a more-subtle Blue-Winged Olive. I tie it on and make delicate casts. Nothing.

I paw through the box some more, and then I see it: the Mop Fly— the chartreuse trout-killer that triggers something guttural in both stocked and wild fish. I'm convinced the Mop Fly will take this fish. I will cast to the head of the pool, where it will plop in pebble-like; then I will strip twice and hook the trout. I'll land it and then gawk at it for a few seconds, with the Mop Fly hanging from its jaw. Then I'll release it and watch it sheepishly pick its way back to the depths of the pool.

Then I think of the amazing rise I just saw a few minutes ago in this oil painting of a trout pool. The image is already delightfully seared into my brain.

So what more does this trout need to give me? I ponder the question for a moment.

Not a damn thing. My tank is beyond full. It's bursting.

Unshackled by the need to fish this pool, I reel up my line and absorb this lovely spot for another few minutes. Then I scramble up the trail to the dirt road and follow it higher and higher, until it eventually turns away from the stream.

The Last of the Woodsmen

The woods that continue far beyond our 14 acres, covering entire mountains and valleys and shadowing rivers and lakes, are typical of the Catskills: understated and sturdy. A writer named T. Morris Longstreth accurately described them in a 1918 travel guide about the region: "There have been no strokes of geologic lightning to rend it into stupefying gulfs. All is blended, suave. It is meant for those who will look twice."

The woodlands here literally keep the mountains together. Their roots grip the soil, which in turn retain the rainwater and snowmelt that represent the savings accounts of our trout rivers. In the clear-cutting days of the 19th century, without forests to control runoff, rivers became muddy, silty torrents. When the trees eventually recolonized, so did the trout. In other words: no trees, no trout.

If there is one person I know who is both of and from these sturdy forests—a living Ent from Tolkien or the Celtic Green Man, protector of the old ways of the woods, it is my neighbor Tim, who lives up the road in a small wooden cabin.

Tim was born in 1961. I know this because it says so on his headstone. Tim is very much alive; he's just planning ahead. The headstone sits in a peaceful, carefully mowed corner of his 50-acre property. A stand of 60-foot-tall white spruce trees planted by his grandfather whisper nearby, and behind that you can hear the low gurgle of a tributary of the six-foot-wide stream. Next to Tim's

are the headstones of his late parents, Marian and Tom, and his
sister Colleen, who succumbed to brain cancer a few years ago at
the age of 47. Their ashes are all buried here.

I remember the first time Mimi and I saw Tim. It was dead
winter, and we were standing in the road, gazing at the cabin for
the first time. Three feet of snow covered the surrounding woods,
with drifts from the town plow piled nearly four feet high. Down
the road he came on foot; bearded and solid, wooden walking staff
in hand, green hooded sweatshirt pulled tight around a Carhartt
cap, dungarees with a few patches, and insulated knee-high rubber
boots. He had the comfortable gait of a man who virtually lived
in those boots.

Just as he passed, I said to him, "Cold enough for you?"

Never stopping and with the muffled thud of his staff striking the road through an inch or two of fresh snow, he replied cheerfully, "Aww, not so bad." Then he kept walking until he was out of sight.

When we got back in the car, the radio said it was eight degrees.

When we first bought our cabin, Tim's mother and father were still alive and lived next door to Tim in a pretty cottage converted from a barn. His grandmother Helen, today well into her 90s and now with her son in South Carolina, lived in the next farmhouse over. Just a little up the road, Tim's cousin Eric owns a 400-acre beef cattle farm. Generations living on the same road, which by the way is named after the family.

The weekend we first moved in, Helen and Marian walked down our driveway to introduce themselves and welcome us. They told us about the history of the cabin: Helen's late husband, Stanley, built it and rented it to hunters before eventually selling it to one of the regulars. The wood used in its construction came from the sawmill they ran just up the road. It closed in 1970 and was eventually dismantled. The forest has since reclaimed the site. After chatting for a few more minutes, they both said to let them know if we needed anything, and their offer had a genuineness to it. Helen then handed us the extra set of keys to the cabin entrusted to her by the former owners.

"You probably want these back," she said.

Mimi took the keys, considered them for a few seconds, and then handed them back to Helen. She said, "You should keep them just in case of an emergency."

Helen smiled, and after that we were pretty much accepted as extended family.

I have since come to learn the term *neighbor* seems to carry more weight than in the suburbs where I live. There's a credo here that neighbors watch out for each other a bit more—probably because the nearest fire or police station is miles away and the closest hospital is nearly a half-hour drive. Meanwhile back at home, I do little more than wave to my neighbors, many of whom I've never actually met.

Over those first few years, we would often stop by and visit Tim's parents or Helen and wind up sitting at the kitchen table and talking for a long time. We'd talk about the weather, or we'd learn about various cousins or nieces and nephews we had never met or hear past stories about our cabin. It felt like we had stepped back in time into some lost cultural phenomenon. I half expected to see the milk truck rumble past or the *Saturday Evening Post* lying on the kitchen table next to the latest issue of *Collier's*. We'd see Tim occasionally, usually when he got home from the stone quarry where he worked. We'd wave, and he'd wave back.

At some point I must have mentioned to Tim's parents that I was interested in exploring the local woods because I was soon encouraged to join Tim on one of his hikes. It turned out he did these frequently and knew intimately the many hundreds of acres of surrounding woodlands. So I joined him one day, and after that we began hiking regularly. I would show up at his house, usually on a Sunday morning when I knew he wasn't working, and knock on his door. Tim would be ready to go with his rubber boots and trusty five-foot hiking staff made of hard maple worn smooth around the handle.

Then he'd ask where I wanted to go. I would pick a direction and say, "How about this way?" Then Tim would lead, and I'd follow. At first, we walked our 14 acres. Tim would point out trees and shrubs and mushrooms and note their natural history or local use or edibility. For example: I learned you can make whistles out of the wood of the striped maple (also called whistlewood); the sap of jewelweed treats poison ivy; and there's a species of edible mushroom that grows on the property that turns blue when you slice it open. My contribution to the hikes was noting the calls of birds, though Tim knew most of them already.

We then followed networks of old logging roads that would take us deep into the forest. We traveled through mature stands of maple, ash, and beech; into dark groves of hemlock; and across ferny bottomlands with springs flowing down from adjacent hillsides. Sometimes, Tim would stop, crouch down, and drink from them. I would keep to my always-prefilled aluminum water bottle, admittedly feeling a little citified about using it.

Occasionally we would come to an overlook with a view of one of the surrounding mountains. "Where are we?" I would ask.

The GPS in rubber boots would then point to one section of the mountain and say, "That's the back of your land; Eric's land starts over there, and mine is down there."

It still just looked like a green mountain to me.

For the most part, these hikes were quiet ambles. Besides birds, most of the wildlife we saw included various amphibians—redspotted newts, American toads, or wood frogs that would respectively crawl or hop away from us. Sometimes we'd spook a deer, which would snort loudly, then bound away with impressive leaps.

One time we startled a black bear sow and her three cubs in some overgrown logging land just above my property line. The sow rushed into a nearby thicket sounding like a runaway boulder crashing through the countryside. Meanwhile all three cubs scrambled up a pine tree—you could hear their long claws cleaving into the bark. They kept climbing higher and higher until they were 30 feet up, then 40, then 50, each one on top of the other. They say never climb a tree to escape a black bear, and based on that performance, I concur. You will most assuredly be outclimbed and ultimately lose. We realized we still had the mother bear nearby, so making as much noise as we could—another bear safety tip—we got the hell out of there. That happened several years ago, but we still remind each other about the experience on nearly every hike.

Occasionally, Tim would stop and point to certain trees. They could be 200 yards from his house or two miles, sometimes much farther. And there carved into the trunk were his initials along with a distant year—usually from when he was a teenager. Along with these carvings, scattered through his property, impressive rock cairns Tim built, five and six feet high, rose from the hillsides like totems. Clearly these woods had been his playground growing up. Today, they are his source of energy and income. He quit his job at the stone quarry several years ago and now lives off the land. He cuts firewood from the forest to feed his woodstove and heat his home—no small feat because, in January, temperatures can hover at around zero degrees for weeks at a time. Indeed, there are stacks of drying firewood scattered throughout Tim's property in various stages of seasoning.

He cuts stone from some of the outcroppings in the woods and sells them as pavers to a local stone yard. I've seen him take on rocks the size of a sports car and, with a gas-powered stone saw and crowbar, slice through them like a spiral ham until little is left but a small pile of rubble. His cousin Eric maintains a small rock quarry on his own property, and sometimes Tim helps him cut stone there. At the end of the work day, he comes off the mountain, covered in rock dust and looking like a sculpture of himself.

Besides these two extractive activities, Tim makes his own maple syrup, something I've helped him with a few times over the years. If you've never watched 40 gallons of water boil down into one, let's just say it is not an activity for the impatient. But I can't think of a nicer way to spend a day or two outdoors in late February or early March, when, for the first time, you can feel winter ease its grip on the land. There is hope in the sunlight; it gives off tangible warmth, and the light of day lingers just a little longer. Sometimes, there's still a foot of snow on the ground; other times just a few patches of corn snow remain in the shady lees of trees and rocks.

Besides the obvious labor of hauling and boiling, you find yourself at the whims of the sugar maple, whose rising sap can feel as temperamental as a rising trout. Not only is air temperature a factor—both daytime highs and nighttime lows—so is wind direction and direct sunlight and other vagaries. These cause some trees to stingily give up their sap in the slowest of drips, while others yield it in delightful trickles.

One time, Mimi and Finn helped out. All went well except toward the end of the day, when we found a drowned red squirrel in one of the sap buckets that had apparently slipped while trying to get a drink. We poured out the contents, cleaned the bucket, and continued our work. Tim said it occasionally happens. The next week at school, Finn told his first-grade class all about how he helped make maple syrup at his cabin. Somehow over the course of the day, the story began to mutate among his classmates. By the time we picked Finn up from school that afternoon, one of his buddies ran up to us and said, "Finn told us about the *giant dead rat* you found when you were making maple syrup!"

Drowned squirrels (or rats) aside, I will say this about Tim's maple syrup: Rendering it the traditional way over a wood fire imbibes into it a subtle smokiness that I have yet to taste in any other. Never, and I mean never, has a pancake tasted so good as when it is smothered in it.

Despite my brief work shifts, Tim's syrup production relies largely on a labor force of one. And with the unpredictability of sap and its flow, some seasons are better than others. On a recent year, which was a good one, he made 20 gallons. Before you say "*Only* 20 gallons?" know that this required gathering, hauling, and boiling no less than 800 gallons of liquid. He sells it mostly through word of mouth and a hand-painted sign he hangs in front of his barn. Tim hasn't made any syrup for the past two seasons— repeated ice storms encased the ground and kept his gathering pipes frozen and unusable one year. The next, he decided to give the sugar maples a rest.

Tim doesn't hunt or fish, though he eats plenty of venison thanks to a few friends who hunt his property each fall and split the meat with him. When Eric butchers one of his cows, Tim gets a cut, too. He raises chickens but got sick of eating eggs, so he sells the occasional dozen to neighbors. His vegetable garden is a showpiece, nurtured through copious amounts of cow manure from Eric's farm. He grows broccoli, kale, spinach, lettuce, pull beans, kidney beans, beets, peas, squash, sugar-sweet carrots, tomatoes, garlic, onions, potatoes, raspberries, and pumpkins. He cans what he doesn't immediately eat. He stopped growing corn because a bear kept scaling the fence and flattening the entire crop—usually the night before he was ready to harvest it. With his permission, I scale his rhubarb patch each spring and bake a few strawberry rhubarb pies. If it's a good apple year, he makes cider from a mechanical press his grandfather built. Tim frequently shares some of his harvest with me. In exchange, I present him with bass fillets, smoked trout, or jars of pickled shad.

Our hikes continue, though the past two years we have only gone once or twice each season. We pledge to remedy this. During our last hike, he took me to two ponds I had never seen before. Both were dug by the landowners. One had a swimming dock; the other was stocked by one of the local kids with a dozen yellow perch. It was only 30 feet across but 15 feet deep according to Tim. The young conservationist hopes to have created his own personal perch hole.

During that hike, we lamented the impending loss of some of the forest's most common trees. An aphid-like insect called the woolly adelgid from Asia has already destroyed hundreds of thousands of acres of hemlocks throughout the eastern United States. Just a few miles away on the Delaware, you can see hillsides covered with yellowing or graying hemlocks affected by the adelgid, which literally sucks the tree dry of its sap. Two years ago, I spotted adelgid—revealed by small cottony spots on the ends of branches—on one of my hemlocks. I told my forester friend Paul about it, who told me not to panic, that it will probably take at least a decade or two for most of my hemlocks to succumb. Because treating hundreds of trees is not an option, there's little I can do except watch to see what types of trees will replace them and hope that a few survive. Another Asian insect called the emerald ash borer has the potential to kill some 8 billion ash trees in North America, according to some estimates. Already, many local landowners are logging their stands of ash before the borer gets to them first. Tim remembers when Dutch elm disease killed many of the elm trees he grew up with.

Before the conversation got too bleak, we came to a particularly beautiful grove of tall and healthy hard maples mixed with some basswood and hornbeam. The clouds gave way to sun, and shafts of light filtered down to us. We stopped for a few minutes to rest. All seemed as it should be, so we moved on.

Eventually we came to the paved road, which always feels slightly jarring. If a car passes, even more so. We walked until we came to Tim's cabin. As we usually do, we both agreed it was a fine hike and then parted ways. Tim had chores to do—he always does. I had trout to catch. I later saw him heading back into the woods with his familiar gait, the old guard watching over the mortar that holds these streams and rivers together.

August 28: I replay the request over and over in my head like a favorite song: "Can you get those big fish out of the pond, Steve?"

"Why, sure I can, Tom."

Tim's dad has a problem: The carp that a neighbor introduced into his half-acre bass pond a few years ago have gotten too big and are starting to wreck the place. They are uprooting aquatic weeds and muddying up the bottom. If only he knew someone, anyone, who could catch them and get them out of there.

My friend Rich and I show up with our seven-weight fly rods rigged with stout ten-pound leaders. Tied to the ends are Glo Bugs—a bright-orange puffball of a fly that in Alaska is supposed to imitate a salmon egg. Here it will have to mimic canned corn, which we plan to use for chum.

Tom is sitting outside on his picnic table, fiddling with a birdhouse. His ever-present mug of coffee sits within arm's reach. He's wearing his usual red suspenders, flannel shirt, and green work pants. He greets us with a boisterous "Hey!"

Marian weeds in the flower garden by the front door of their farmhouse. At this angle, she looks neck-deep in day lilies. She greets us with a cheerful hello, then says something to Tom about coming in for lunch a little later. She always calls him Thomas, which I think is nice.

We briefly discuss our simple strategy: Rich and I will throw a few handfuls of corn near a drop-off in the pond, then lay out our fly lines with our Glo Bugs in the middle of the chum and wait to see what happens.

I scatter the corn and watch it settle over maybe ten square feet of bottom. Then we roll-cast our Glo Bugs and let them slowly sink until they rest among the kernels.

We chat with Tom. It's been a good summer—warm but not too dry. Corn is high. They'll do the next cutting of hay soon. Probably lots of apples in a few weeks.

A hush falls over us. A submarine in the form of a 15-pound carp ghosts in from the deeper water and approaches the chum. A second one follows, maybe just a few pounds smaller.

Both fish sidle past the corn, casing it like a liquor store they plan on sticking up later. They stop, K-turn in the shallows, and return to deeper water.

We wait again but this time only briefly. The larger fish reappears, but this time it is snout-down, vacuuming up corn kernels two and three at a time. You can see its pinkish lips extending down like a hose. With each kernel it sucks in, a little puff of silt comes up with it. The second fish has joined in, too, tentatively cruising the periphery but dipping down once every few inches to slurp up another corn kernel.

Both fish draw closer to our flies. Rich's is closest to the big fish. We can see the orange of the Glo Bug among the yellow corn. Rich, Tom, and I are now all crouched over. Waist-high water lilies that surround the pond act as a sort of blind that hopefully will prevent the carp from seeing too much of us.

I look for the fly again, but it's gone.

"Rich, he's got it."

Rich keeps the rod low and sets the hook with multiple jabs like he's coming tight to a tarpon. The fish shakes its head back and forth once or twice. Each carp fights differently. I have caught some that do little more than roll on their sides and gurgle in surrender. Others are sheer brutes.

This one is clearly no surrendering gurgler. It powers to the far side of the pond, taking yards of line and sending up a swath of muck and corn kernels. The second carp immediately flees into the security of deep water. Rich's reel shrieks like it has a bonefish on the other end. He chases the fish down the pond to make sure fly line doesn't wind up tangled in the water lilies.

Tom enjoys the whole show. He keeps back but smiles while Rich wrestles the big fish closer. When it gets a few feet away, he whistles and says quietly, "Whoa, that's a big one."

Then Rich reaches down and grabs the fish by the gill plate and hauls it up the bank. It lays there in the grass pumping its gills.

He unhooks it, and he and Tom decide to sit and talk while I throw out more chum and await another carp. It doesn't take long. The second fish returns and within minutes sucks up my fly. I jab the hook and begin my own wrestling match while Rich and Tom watch. Before long, a second fish—maybe eight pounds—lies next to the first.

I ask Tom what he wants to do with the fish. Carp are an invasive species and reviled, at least here in the United States. In some states it's illegal to release them alive. I figure Tom, being a farmer, will calmly walk over and dispatch them and then bury them in his garden or something.

But he doesn't. He just looks at the two carp still gasping in the grass.

So I offer, "Tom, do you want me to throw them in the woods somewhere?"

The smile leaves his face and is replaced by a look of pain.

"Oooo, I wish you wouldn't," he says wincing.

And then I realize that it's the carps' lucky day. I lay each fish in a galvanized tub I borrow from Tom. Then I get my car, and Rich and

I drive them to an undisclosed spot that I know already has plenty of carp in it, and I let the fish go. They flounder in the water for a few minutes seemingly stunned. But being carp, they get over the trauma of the last hour pretty quickly and swim off.

I drive back and tell Tom we took care of the fish. He smiles and thanks me.

In memory of Tom (1931–2005),
Marian (1939–2008),
and Rich (1940–2014)

Stream Walks, Night Walks

Ever since Finn could take his first steps, we have spent many hours together, sloshing through the six-foot wide-stream. We call these simply "stream walks," and they have become a sort of institution. For the first few years, I would hold Finn's hand, and he would slip and slide along. Fast-forward to our most recent walk, when he reached the top of the property long before I did. He bounded along, periodically calling, "C'mon, Dad," like I was an old family dog struggling to keep up. By the time I got there, he stood thigh-deep in the last pool ready to dunk his head under.

The perfect stream walk is done without fishing tackle, which I learned early on only serves as a distraction. This is not the time for stalking a six-inch brook trout holding in a pool the size of a kitchen sink. Instead, I choose to happily galumph along, wearing wading shoes and shorts, splashing water everywhere, especially on myself. Every catchable trout flees under the nearest rock, wondering what the hell just happened. It's liberating in a way. After spending most of the spring clutching a fly rod and creeping around like a great blue heron, it's oddly fun to unabashedly spook every catchable trout in the creek. And maybe it's good for them, too, kind of like an air-raid drill for when a merganser shows up.

The only trout we target during stream walks are fry that we scoop up in an aquarium net. To do this, Finn and I construct mini rock weirs, and then one of us chases the fish downstream, where the net awaits. We place the trout in a clear plastic bucket

with some stream water and see if we can tell the rainbows from the brookies. It's not as easy as you think. Bonus is the occasional sculpin, which always looks more aggravated than scared when you drop it in among the trout.

Along with fish-netting, stream walks are proving grounds to hone the time-honored skill of catch-and-release frogging. Two varieties live in the stream. Pickerel frogs have dual racing stripes down their backs; green frogs are more two-toned. Both are lightning fast. In *Fishless Days, Angling Nights*, Sparse Gray Hackle wrote, "Boys and frogs have gone together ever since there were boys and frogs." I am happy to report this still holds true. Finn is a championship-caliber frogger, and his stalk-and-pounce method is something to behold.

Flipping streamside rocks looking for critters combines the excitement of digging for pirate treasure with panning for gold. Booty comes in the form of various aquatic insects, which go into the clear bucket with the trout fry, where they scuttle about. Crayfish prompt real excitement as they paddle from rock to rock in a game of hide and seek, with Finn or me giving chase. Sometimes they shoot into a stronger tongue of current and are gone, thus winning the game.

The absolute gold-medal-critter prize goes to the spring salamander, the jumbo-sized amphibian that unfortunately wound up in my water pipe a few years back. In the stream, they are as elusive as a snow leopard. We look for certain-sized flat rocks lying half in and half out of the water. The best ones lie close to one of the many icy seeps along the stream. The rock can't be flush to the bottom; it must rest on smaller rocks to allow for hiding places underneath. Catching is a two-person job. After the proper rock is found, one person lifts, while the other gets ready to grab. Here's the challenge: When the rock comes up, it almost always leaves a puff of mud or silt exactly where a salamander might be hiding, so you have to wait a second or two for the water to clear, and then—if you are lucky—you might see a flash of pinkish-orange. Reach in slowly, and see if you can corner your prize. Frequently, the salamander gets away, slipping and sliding beneath rock after rock until it vanishes. Other times you are rewarded with eight inches of sinewy amphibian that you briefly admire before letting it go.

Though most of what we encounter is aquatic, there are other visitors to the stream, too. During a stream walk when Finn was four years old, he stopped suddenly along the streambank where some tall grasses grew. Without saying a word, he pointed in front of him with a smile on his face like he just saw one of Santa's elves. I walked over and looked. No more than three feet away from him was a curled-up fawn that may have been two days old. I am generally not fond of deer, as they eat my plantings, but seeing this spotted newborn and my four-year-old son staring at each other was beyond adorable. We left, but Finn insisted we check back after lunch. By then the fawn was long gone, undoubtedly ushered away by mom, who probably watched us from behind a nearby tree the entire time.

On the hottest days of summer, where the stream is the closest thing we get to air conditioning, we go on what we call "old-fashioned" stream walks, meaning just bathing suits and water shoes, no shirts. We often stop and sit in the stream, usually where water sluices between two boulders. Finn, thicker-skinned than me, always goes in first. I follow, shuddering when the chilled flow hits the small of my back. But after that initial shock, the stream feels wonderful purling around me. Then we get up and slosh to the next pool and do it again. When we reach the top of the property, we walk all the way down the dirt road to the cabin, feeling like Huck Finn and Tom Sawyer. Mimi joins in sometimes. Other times she sits on the porch with a book, and we report our various catches and adventures when we return. I can't think of a more pleasant way to spend time on a trout stream in the summer. Don't tell anyone this, but at times, it may even be better than . . . fishing. There, I said it.

Then there are night walks. No, these are not done in the stream but on the dirt road that runs in front of the cabin leading to the Delaware. We bring flashlights just in case, but the best walks are done in full darkness. They often begin with a pause at the bottom of the driveway, where you step out from the shadows of the woods, then look up at a full, unfettered view of the night sky. According to maps that show light pollution, we are mercifully far away from any urban centers and their luminescent stains. When guests stay overnight, I walk them down the driveway using a dim headlamp I keep pointed to the ground. Then I shut it off and tell them to look up. Above them, a mural of the heavens stares down—the swath of the Milky Way, Jupiter, Venus, and depending on the time of year Saturn or Mars. Maybe a shooting star streaks past. Quiet "oohs" and "aahs" sometimes accompany this celestial show; other times, just silent awe or even reverence. The lonely call of a barred owl or the yip of a coyote might echo from one of the surrounding mountains—a particularly nice touch when it happens.

If there are kids in the group, I will then sometimes call for a quick game of "satellite throw-down." The rules are simple: First one to see a satellite wins. It's surprising how few of them have ever seen one—grown-ups included. Just look for a star that moves silently across the night sky, and you've got it. If it blinks, it's a plane. Winner gets a high-five.

Then the walk begins in earnest down the dirt road. Depending on the time of year, the sounds from the woods range from quiet, particularly in August, when the six-foot-wide stream runs at just a gurgle, to deafening, when thousands of spring peepers are at their friskiest in May and June. The frogs call from a spongy hillside next to the road.

Spring peepers are as elusive to see as they are loud. First of all, despite their booming call, they are tiny—approximately fingernail-sized. Second, they seem to be ventriloquists, particularly when many call together as one. Their collective wall of sound disorients; you approach one over here, but it turns out to be over there. Then when you finally think you have it cornered, it promptly shuts up. Despite my best attempts with a headlamp and quiet stalking, I have only actually seen peepers a handful of times. I can personally vouch that they are impossibly small, and one wonders how they can pack so many decibels into such a diminutive body type.

Like finding a spring salamander on a stream walk, the night-walk critter prize goes to the tiny glowworm, which is the larval form of the firefly. The winged adults put on an aerial pyrotechnic show in the late spring that can astound, with many hundreds of performers emitting rapid-fire blinks and comet-like streaks over nearby farm fields and clearings. The glowworm is far more subtle, and one's night vision needs to be honed to detect one. They seem to prefer crawling in the loam beneath high, wet grass. First, you see a subtle green pulse along the roadside. You approach, and it shuts off. You wait, and it pulses again. You draw closer. It stops. Then you stop. Sometimes you need to wait for five or six pulses before you are close enough to turn on a flashlight and spot the actual source—a flattened, dark, multilegged millipede-like bug no more than a half-inch long. Picking one up apparently does not frighten it, as it continues to pulse light in your hand.

Walking back to the cabin, I often break the rule of minimal lights by scanning the road for snakes that I assume are there trying to absorb the last bits of thermal heating from the sun. We usually spot garters and ringnecks. One year, I found a beautiful baby milk snake. It laid there calmly, camouflaged in grays and browns like a warplane. I pointed it out to Mimi and Finn, then thought I would show off by picking it up. It bit surprisingly hard.

The campfire always seems particularly inviting when you return from a night walk. It is home base, and you have made it back safely. It's time to toss on another log or two and tell stories about glowworms or other creatures (I happen to know a good salamander story).

For us bug geeks, campfires at the cabin can sometimes erupt into moments of great excitement. This happens whenever a giant moth starts buzzing around the light outside the porch. The first thing you see is an enormous shadow, then an apparition of ghostly wing flaps. If you are lucky, one will alight on the siding, allowing for close-up observation. Several varieties of outsized moths have visited, including various sphinx moths, whose bark camouflage makes them virtually vanish when they land on a tree. Then there are the three members of the otherworldly-sounding *Saturniidae* family: luna moths, with their pale-green wings and trailing Victorian tails, and cecropia and polyphemus moths, known for their wing spots that look like giant staring eyeballs. All of these beings, from calling owls to glowing worms, give the night a sacred and rare beauty that I feel privileged to experience.

I suppose there may be a time when Finn might look at things like stream walks and catching glowworms as babyish. Before I know it, he'll probably be trying to kick Mimi and me out of the cabin for the weekend so he can hang out with his college buddies. Until then—and beyond—I'll continue to walk the stream, stare at the night sky, and catch crayfish with the enthusiasm of a 12-year-old and hope that I pass this trait along to him as a great gift.

September 10: Sometime after trout season plays out, I will get an e-mail from my friend Mark, who owns a cottage on the river about two miles from the cabin. After a line or two about weather or water levels, the e-mail will conclude with a simple question: "Meat this weekend?"

This is not cryptic code; it simply means "Let's fish for our dinner."

And today is that day.

I pick up Mark midmorning. He brings an ancient spinning rod of unknown vintage; an old vest with a few spinners, plugs, and jigs stuffed into the pockets; and a bottle of seltzer. I have requisitioned a spinning outfit from Finn, but the reel sounds a little raspy, like the main bearing might be about to go.

But for the fishing at hand, our tackle feels perfectly appropriate.

We drive to where Mark's johnboat is stored under the deck of the house of another neighbor, who kindly grants both docking and launching privileges. We climb underneath and extract it.

She is a beauty and a genuine gift from the river gods. Ten feet long and made of aluminum, it may weigh less than the overstuffed tackle box I lug along. Mark found it one day capsized and wedged in a logjam following a mini river flood. After he recovered it, he scrupulously inquired with various upstream neighbors, but no one knew its origin, so the ancient maritime law of salvage kicked in, which is a nautical way of saying "finders keepers." Now he is the captain.

We place in the boat the two fishing rods; my giant tackle box; lifejackets; two oars; the seltzer; and, almost reluctantly, a cooler and landing net. I say reluctantly because, for some reason, our fishing success is nearly always better if we forget these last two items.

Launching Mark's boat has its challenges. With lightness comes instability, and the ten-footer is no exception to this rule of physics. After

Mark settles in at the stern, I carefully take the bench in the middle to assume motorman's responsibilities. I gently shove off, and five feet from the bank, we nearly capsize. We lean hard to starboard to right our ship, laughing at our near-calamity. Laughter continues while I row upriver. At the top of a slow and deep eddy, we begin our first drift. We glide slowly past a submerged field of large boulders in water that gradually deepens. We cast randomly. Our selection of lures has evolved over the years. One season, I was sold on plastic "tube jigs," which had become all the rage among professional bass anglers. They were black and cylindrical, with tentacles dangling off at one end. Mark called them "turd jigs." They fooled a few smallmouth and a walleye or two, though recently they seem to have lost their charm. One time, Mark insisted on using a bright-pink bucktail because he caught a big bonefish on it in the Bahamas 30 years ago. No bonefish that day, but a fallfish and a rock bass latched on. We have cast propeller lures that churn the surface like miniature outboard motors, crankbaits resembling dying crayfish, and slim plastic worms to imitate sea lamprey larvae. Some have worked; many have not. We often make fun of whichever lure the other one is using, part of a tradition of banter that has evolved over the years of fishing this spot together.

Another unwritten rule is that whoever hooks the first fish gets to spout off insufferably like they were Izaak Walton. Soon, Mark boats a 13-inch smallmouth that hit a gold spinner.

He lands the fish, turns to me, and says, "You know, smallmouth here really like gold, but you've got to be an expert to fish a spinner just right. I'd show you how, but you probably wouldn't get it."

I'm tempted to scuttle or self-capsize, but I refrain. Instead, I keep casting.

As we float through the pool, we sometimes reminisce about previous glory: the time when Mark caught a massive chain pickerel that puked up a recently swallowed nine-inch trout; or two years ago, when big smallmouth crushed our plastic worms on nearly every drift (forgot the net of course); or the walleye we've caught and how delicious they tasted.

And other times: when we saw a guide boat anchored in the tail-out of the pool, hooking walleye seemingly on every other cast. They released them, which made it worse—particularly because we were catching none. Provided they are in season and are of legal size, walleye are two delicious fillets motorized by a tail. Mechanically tossing back legal walleye one after another smacked of tycoons lighting cigars with $100 bills. Of course, they may have already taken their limit and were now catch-and-release fishing, but that is beside the point.

Walleye fascinate us both. There are rumors of 30-inch 10-pounders caught in this very pool. On nearly every trip, one of us gets a follow from a nicer fish. We see it ghosting behind the lure in the clear water. Almost invariably, they veer away at the last second.

This might prompt a mini lecture from the other angler: "It's Saturday, right? Saturday walleyes are followers. Thursday walleye are eaters."

I hook a 16-inch smallmouth that has grabbed a plastic worm fished "wacky" style—a trick straight out of the Bassmasters Tournament Trail. You hook the worm dead center and let it drift slowly so both sides slowly undulate. As I fight the fish, I explain to Mark that I realized the barometer was rising slightly, so of course I chose that lure. But it's a big-fish technique definitely not for beginners.

The bass jumps once, then dives repeatedly under the johnboat, prompting more fear of capsizing. Mark surges with the net and deftly scoops it up. I bleed the fish and place it in the cooler. An hour later, with no more hits, we decide to row ashore.

Back at Mark's I fillet the smallmouth and present it to his wife, Deb, for their dinner that night. Then we all sit outside and over a late-afternoon beer watch the river go by. Mark and I speculate whether the fishing might have been better if we started earlier in the day, or maybe one of these times we need to finally fish at night for walleye—which purportedly gorge after the sun goes down. Something to think about for the next time we meat on the river.

Coming and Going

The straight-line distance between the cabin and my home in New Jersey is a little over 120 miles. Depending on when I leave (day and time); which route I take; and, most importantly, what sort of distractions come up along the way, it takes me between two-and-a-half and eight hours each way.

Having made the trip back and forth literally hundreds of times, I can say without hesitation that the absolute worst time to head up is on a Friday night after work. This is when bumper-to-bumper traffic is virtually ensured for the first half of the trip. Yet, I also say with equal conviction that my absolute favorite time to drive up is also on a Friday night after work. If this makes no sense, it's because you've never slowly rolled down the driveway underneath the spruce trees at 9:00 at night after fighting three or four hours of traffic. If it's spring or early summer, you can still see a few slivers of light left in the western sky. After you unpack the car, you open the windows on the porch, pour a post-drive cocktail, and then melt to the rush of the stream. What traffic?

I have two main options for travel routes. One is faster but consists mostly of highway driving. I speed along with my fellow motorists, many of whom look like they, too, are rushing to and from various upstate and downstate vacation spots. To my right, a minivan labors with a fleet of bicycles hanging from bike racks. On my left, a mud-splattered pickup truck with tinted windows and an ATV in the bed howls past (please don't take the same

exit as me). I rarely go this way because it feels too much like a straight-up commute—in other words, mindless and soulless.

Instead, I travel mostly two-lane state roads that I find far more interesting. There I can observe the comings and goings of small towns, stop when I feel like it at various points of interest, and maybe squeeze in some fishing and birding along the way.

On state roads, I can track the success of various roadside businesses—farm stands, hot dog trucks, diners, and shot-and-a-beer roadhouses. I have watched some establishments turn over three or four times since we bought the cabin. When a new owner hangs strings of plastic multicolored pennants proclaiming a grand opening, I always root for success. If they close, I lament their loss.

I pass through villages and hamlets and see signs for tricky trays, penny socials, and firemen's pancake breakfasts. Though I've yet to buy a ticket, just knowing that I could if I wanted to makes me feel welcome.

We do have a few traditional food stops. If we dally and wind up heading to the cabin on a Saturday morning, we make sure to visit a bagel shop we discovered in northern New Jersey mainly for one reason: bacon. They seem to pile it by the pound onto their egg sandwiches, thus answering the question, can there ever be too much bacon? (The answer is clearly no.) Stopping there for breakfast often takes care of lunch for the day (not to mention your sodium intake for the week). Then there is the pizza joint in a Pennsylvania river town that makes a surprisingly decent pie. I am usually suspicious of any pizza made more than an hour's drive from New York City, but this one is the exception. They must secretly truck in city tap water—long-believed to be the secret ingredient to a perfect crust.

There have been other culinary surprises. One time while driving home, we decided to stop at an out-of-the-way roadside food stand just a few miles from the cabin. There, listed on its chalkboard of daily specials, was something completely unexpected: the knish—the quintessential Coney Island boardwalk food. It seemed so audacious to feature such regional fare—like a Jewish deli serving chicken-fried steak—that I immediately felt the need to order one. It turned out to be the best knish I ever tasted, with a crunchy but chewy rind and a fluffy, creamy potato filling with just the right amount of black pepper.

Nonfood stops include a few mom-and-pop tackle shops, one of which still sells loose shad darts—nowadays a rarity—and the occasional antique store, where Mimi inevitably ferrets out some cabin essential. She recently unearthed a vintage wire magazine rack that went straight to the outhouse. How could we have ever lived without one?

In spring, distractions abound. Driving past no fewer than a half-dozen heavily stocked trout streams along the way without stopping is an exercise in restraint. And I often fail at it. As much as I love to catch and release wild trout in the six-foot-wide stream and in the Delaware, I am an absolute meat hog of stocked trout, which I release directly into my smoker. This is guilt-free fishing because I know that, within the next week or so, a hatchery truck will back up to the closest pool and dump in another hundred or so.

Sometimes, usually on solo trips to the cabin, I stop for "just a few casts," which winds up burning a half-day to fill up my chain stringer. But later, after five hours in my smoker with a couple of panfuls of applewood, it is oh so worth it.

With Mimi and Finn in the car, I usually keep driving, as they are not as enthralled with hatchery trout as I am, though I do make it a point to name each stream and the quota of trout it receives. Maybe twice a season, if I happen to have a spinning rod in the car already rigged up, I'll lurch into a turnoff and insist on a few quick casts. If something flashes behind the lure or strikes and misses, that's often good enough. I can fill my smoker next time.

Roadside birding, on the other hand, I can usually do without straying more than five feet from my car. For example, at a certain gas station along a rural New Jersey road, I can pick off at least five or six migratory songbirds while I fill my tank—usually red-eyed vireos, yellowthroats, ovenbirds, yellow warblers, and wood thrushes. But I've been surprised by indigo buntings and scarlet tanagers, too. A few miles past there, if I roll down the window and drive slowly past a particular overgrown field, I often hear a prairie warbler singing. My ace birding friends say its rising buzzy song sounds like a flying saucer taking off.

Two birds once taught me the value of not rushing during these back-and-forth trips. I was heading home late in the afternoon and got stuck at a long traffic light on a bridge that crossed the Delaware. There was construction, and the light controlled one-way traffic, so you had to wait while the opposing traffic passed. I sat in the car, grumbling something about "losing time," when I saw them coming from downriver. A pair of adult bald eagles approached with great ponderous wing flaps. At the bridge they caught an updraft that sent them soaring leisurely overhead. They banked slowly in the wind, and the sun lit up their white heads and tails. I watched them continue upriver until they became mere specks. The honk of a car startled me, and I looked up to see that the light had already turned green. And that's the last time I complained about not making good time.

When we head home on Sunday afternoons, we occasionally get on the road a little earlier than usual. Maybe the trout fishing is slow or the stream is too cold for a stream walk or Tim isn't available for a hike. When this happens, I sometimes suggest that we stop at some place along the way we always wanted to see but haven't yet. So far, this has included a few antique stores, some historic sites, and a river access that looked promising for small-mouth and shad. And then one time in late September several years back, I suggested, "Hey, let's stop at that old white church."

Mimi knew exactly which one I meant. We had passed it a hundred times. It sat on a hill above the state road and looked like something out of a postcard. It had pretty white clapboard sides and fieldstone walls. A few large white pines stood next to it shading a small peaceful-looking cemetery. The church itself looked like it was no longer regularly used, but the grounds were well-maintained and seemed open to the public, so we stopped there.

We pulled into a grass parking area, which, not surprisingly, was deserted. Finn, age five at the time, immediately got out of the car and began running around the grounds, exploring. Mimi and I walked up a stone path that led up the hill to the church. Then we decided to look at the cemetery. Most of the headstones we saw came from the early to middle 19th century. Of note but not unexpected given the time period, was the number of children buried there—aged six, aged eight, aged ten, et cetera.

I looked up at the church once more and saw its white steeple. In the harsh afternoon light, it now looked stark, almost like an old black-and-white picture. For the first time, I noticed on the hill stumps of old pine trees bleached like bones.

Perhaps it was the loneliness of the place or maybe something else, but I started to get an uneasy feeling. With Finn still running around exploring, I quietly asked Mimi what she thought of the church. As if reading my mind, she admitted that she thought it was on the creepy side.

Then I asked, "Are you getting a weird feeling?"

I barely finished my sentence when she emphatically replied, "Yes."

Time to go.

By now, Finn had run up to the front door of the church. He pulled on it a few times, but it was locked. Then he called over to me and asked if I could hold him up so he could look in the window.

Not wanting to let on that, by now, Mom and Dad were fully creeped out, I reluctantly agreed. I walked over, picked him up, and he and I both peered in the window. The inside of the church looked cold and empty, with just some dusty-looking pews and a bare altar. I put him down and smartly challenged him to a race back to the car. But this time I didn't let him win. In fact, I pretty much left him in the dust. When he caught up, he was saying something about how he didn't know that Daddy could run so fast. By then, I was already starting the car. A few weeks later, we closed the cabin for the winter and forgot all about it.

One day the next spring, we were driving up with Mimi's niece, who was staying with us for the weekend. She had never been to the cabin before and was looking forward to seeing the place for the first time. When we passed the white church, she remarked how pretty it looked on the hill with sun shining down through the pine trees. Finn at this point had been blankly staring out the other window, so Mimi told her niece in a quiet voice how we stopped there last year and how it turned out to be a kind of creepy, lonely place.

That's when Finn immediately said, "We weren't alone."

Mimi and I looked at each other. Already, the hackles on my neck began to stand up in anticipation of what I feared might be coming.

"Uh, what do you mean, Finn?" I asked.

Finn said, "Remember the little girl? The one standing in the church when you held me up?"

Maybe I didn't hear that quite right. "Wait—what?" I asked.

Finn said it again, plainly and clearly, "When you held me up, there was a little girl in the church. *Remember?*"

I should point out that Finn has never had imaginary friends. He never saw fairies in the woods or otherwise made up any fantastical worlds or creatures.

There was a long pause. I tried to keep my eyes on the road but could see Mimi staring at me wide-eyed. Her niece remained silent. All we could hear was the hum of the car engine.

Then I said, "Umm, no Finn, I don't think I remember that," then immediately changed the subject and began babbling about all of the great things we might do at the cabin when we got there. Mimi jumped right in, too. Pretty soon, we were all having a lively debate about the jumping abilities of frogs versus toads or something—anything—to avoid talking about what Finn just said. We never brought it up again—Mimi and I agreed we just didn't want to go there.

All these years later, whenever we drive past the church, I tend to hit the accelerator just a little harder until I can see the white steeple safely in the rearview mirror. Not that we're in a rush or anything.

All of this driving back and forth can frankly be trying, and toward the end of the season, I begin to grow weary of it. But then we spend that final weekend, usually in late October, closing the cabin up for the winter. We drain the water pipes, strip beds, empty and unplug the refrigerator, and pack up my fly-tying gear and tackle. We bring home toys that Finn will probably outgrow by the next year. I set the bucket trap in the crawl space and fill it with RV antifreeze so it will continue to catch mice throughout the winter. Outside, we rake leaves from the maple and ash trees and put away the Adirondack chairs that sat around the campfire since April. Then, finally, we say goodbye to Tim and other neighbors. There's a palpable feeling of sadness. By the time I get home, I have already started missing the drive and its various twists, turns, bumps, and detours.

October 18: *The humidity has finally gone, blown away to distant lands by the last passing cold front. Wander into the shade now, and the air temperature drops by ten degrees.*

In this weaker afternoon sunlight, the river almost looks black. And in it, a single trout rises, winking silver. It holds in the eddy downstream of a long rock slab lying at a 45-degree angle just beneath the water's surface. I spot the rise from a high bank, and a slight feeling of dread comes over me. I think I already know how this scenario will play out.

The six-foot-wide stream closed for the season two weeks ago to protect its spawning brookies, but the Delaware remains open.

Some anglers praise autumn trout fishing for its dearth of fishermen, crisp air, and fall colors. I am not one of these disciples. A melancholy hangs over these woods and mountains, now bird-silent and yellowing with age. What few insects still hatch do so randomly and in sparse numbers. Trout rise indifferently, if at all.

There have been exceptions. The 20-inch rainbow I landed on a four-weight pack rod a few miles from here one rainy afternoon in late September. It rose steadily below a fallen hemlock, and I gasped when I first saw its length and girth.

Fishing aside, I know what else is coming: the steel curtain that is winter up here. Gray, dead, lifeless woods. A cold and silent cabin. No Finn running around outside, catching frogs. No cocktails around the campfire. No hikes with Tim. So there is an urgency as I string up my rod, yank line through the guides, and tug on waders. Cast now or forever hold your peace.

I scramble down the steep bank and slink through tangles of goldenrod and other fading perennials. The sour tang of rotting leaves hangs in the air.

The river runs low and clear, so I wade in as carefully as possible. A line from a Field & Stream *article I read in high school flashes in my head about approaching a rising trout "like you were stalking a gray squirrel." I approach the fish from upstream, trying not to push any sort of wake and staying as low as I can without actually crawling on my hands and knees.*

The trout is not a steady riser. It comes up tentatively maybe once every minute or two. As I draw closer, I scan the river, looking for bugs, but there's no discernable hatch, just minutia in the surface film. So nothing to imitate. Low water. Spooky trout. The feeling of dread persists.

I reach a spot where I can manage a decent cast, albeit a long one, but before I do, I make it a point to stop and behold what's around me. It is undeniably beautiful here. The sky has the deep, rich blue you only see in October; the river sparkles as it continues its way downstream; and the trees covering the mountains that surround this valley are absolutely lit up. I am standing in nothing less than a cathedral.

I strip out line and ready my cast. In anticipation of challenging conditions, I've rigged a 16-foot leader that tapers to 6X, which breaks at less than four pounds of pressure—the lightest tippet I will fish. Some anglers will go down to 7X or even 8X in these conditions. But tippet that thin breaks if you sneeze, and I don't want to play a hooked trout like it's an 800-pound tuna.

The fish continues its random rises. I tie on a size 18 blue-winged olive, one of the few bugs you will still see hatching this late in the season. I begin false casting.

The flow of the river looks uniform and glass smooth, but it deceives. Look closer, and it is a mosaic of conflicting billows of current pushing and pulling at each other. Even a seemingly well-cast fly is subject to its whims. The 8X guys call this "microdrag." And when fussy, rising trout detect it, they say, "I'm no longer hungry."

There are tricks to overcome drag. I decide to throw a slack-line cast, where I wiggle the rod as the fly descends. This sends waves of energy down the line and into the leader and causes the tippet to lay out in little S-curves. This can buy a few precious inches of natural, drag-free float.

I make the cast, and the fly touches down two feet upstream of the fish. I can see slack in the tippet as I hoped and then watch as the fly dead-drifts over the trout. I tense. Nothing happens. I let the fly drift well below the fish, strip it partway back, then pick up the line, and cast again. Once more, all comes together, and the fly lays out and floats just like a real insect.

Nothing.

I decide to wait for the trout to rise again. I strip the fly partway back, then roll-cast it, where I grab it, blow on it a few times to dry, and wait.

And wait.

And wait some more.

This self-fulfilling prophesy has come to pass. The trout is not coming back. It probably spooked on the first cast, as I thought it might. Fall trout are like that.

But come next spring, this same fish, assuming it survives the winter, will gulp and slash at hatching caddis or March browns. And I will be there, casting for it.

I reel up my line and sink the fly in the cork of my rod for the last time. For now, my trout season is over.

The To-Do List

The door on the porch squeaks. I should probably get some WD-40 and spray it. In fact, the door doesn't really close tight unless you slam it. Maybe it's the doorstop, which probably needs replacing again. I'll have to get a new one, but I'll need to cut it down by a half-inch with a hacksaw because the door frame is an irregular size.

There's a paint splotch on the porch that bugs me. It's on the bottom of the door frame that leads inside the cabin. Must have slipped with the roller when we were painting the floor. That was in 2003. Need to buy a small can of cream-colored oil paint and touch it up.

One of these days, I should clean all of the old forest tent caterpillar cocoons wedged between the tops of the jalousie windows. I thought by now they would have been taken by birds for nesting material or fallen off by themselves. Caterpillar silk is tough stuff, I guess. A power washer might do it. I hear you can rent them.

In the main room, I can see some steel wool poking out of the bottom of the paneling near the wood stove, where I once saw a mouse crawl underneath. I should get some floor molding, paint it to match the walls, and hammer it to the wall studs to seal it up once and for all. Actually, I should tear down the paneling altogether and replace it with either beadboard or shiplap. I could stain it nice and dark. And while I'm at it, I'd like to take down the entire ceiling to give the room more of a vaulted, open look. By

doing that, I'd eliminate the crawl space, where I still occasionally hear mice scurrying around. Or maybe they're flying squirrels? Of course, when I pull down the ceiling, I'll probably have to redo all of the wiring because it's just sort of lying around up there by whomever installed it. First, I should read *Wiring for Dummies*, assuming there is such a book.

I still haven't replaced the missing screen on the window in the Walleye Room that's been closed since we bought the place. All I need is a tape measure and a pencil and paper. I think they're in the desk drawer on the porch. Pretty soon, it looks like the roof in the Walleye Room will need replacing because it's almost completely covered in moss. It doesn't leak, so maybe it's fine. I wonder if I could make a thatch roof like an Irish cottage? Something tells me earwigs live in them. Maybe not. Might be time to talk to Tim.

The good news is that I didn't see any sawdust piles on the floor near the door like I did last year. So the carpenter ants—or was it powder post beetles?—presumably succumbed to the bug bomb I unleashed.

Speaking of mice, the ones in the shed are getting cheeky. It's at the point that, when I walk in, I feel like I'm invading their personal space. I sometimes see one or two staring down at me with indignation from one of the roof beams. I used to believe it was better to cede the shed to them rather than have them invade the house. Now I'm considering a zero-tolerance policy regardless of where they might live. A few years ago, I wound up in the hospital with Lyme disease, and last spring I pulled three ticks off Finn, who thankfully is fine. But now we're spraying our clothes with the insecticide Permethrin as a prophylaxis. I've heard you can treat your property for ticks by soaking cotton balls in Permethrin, stuffing them in cardboard tubes, and then leaving them around the property. The mice gather the cotton for nests and thereby expose—and kill—the ticks.

Or I can just use the bucket trap and drown them—both the mice and ticks at the same time. I think I like that method better. I also just read that opossums are sort of tick vacuum cleaners. Any ticks they find on themselves they immediately eat. That's absolutely disgusting, but they have my gratitude. Maybe I could somehow encourage opossums to spend more time around the cabin. Not sure how to do that without attracting bears, too.

I noticed a few trees on the other side of the six-foot-wide stream that finally succumbed to the '06 flood. The glacier of rock and debris that came from upriver buried the crown of their trunks, and I knew it was just a matter of time before they would suffocate. Looks like two ash and a yellow birch. All would make great firewood. I should ask Tim if he could help me take them down. We could divide up the wood.

Speaking of trees, I see that the birch seedlings, some of which are now ten feet tall, have formed a dense thicket that blocks my view of the stream in some places. Maybe I should thin them out a little. I've got a pruning saw in the shed. There's a boxelder, too, that's really taking off. Not sure where it came from. It has to be

15 feet tall already. It looks nice to me, but some people say they are weed trees. Should I take it down, too?

What should I do if I find emerald ash borer on the property? Do I treat my few favorite trees, or do I let them all die? Paul says an arborist can inject individual trees with a chemical that kills the larvae. It costs about $300 per tree and lasts for a few years. There are at least three around the cabin I'd hate to lose, and if they die and fall, they could cause serious damage. Something to think about.

What I don't want to think about is the woolly adelgid and whether it will destroy the hemlock forest, so I won't—at least not for now.

Invasive species can drive you nuts if you let them. The garlic mustard I thought I eradicated last year has come back. Maybe I can convince Finn to pull it again at a nickel a plant. It might cost me five bucks now, but if I wait until next year, I might go broke. The oriental bittersweet returned, too. Definitely need to cut that down before it makes its way up the spruce tree. Forget the honeysuckle thicket next to the driveway and the bishop's weed that now takes up half the hillside. I raise the white flag to them. Plus, I think bishop's weed makes a beautiful ground cover, with its green leaves brushed with white and yellow flowers that hummingbirds love. Guess that's how it got here in the first place—someone thought it looked pretty.

Some of the bigger rocks in the fire pit have cracked. This happens every few years from repeated heating and expanding from campfires. Earlier this season when it got down to the 40s on a few nights, I really stoked up the campfire a few times with armfuls of dry firewood, so I'm sure that didn't help. Need to walk the stream and find some replacements, but I'll avoid anything directly in the water, as I know they can explode when they get hot. I found a beautiful, flat rock maybe three feet long and rectangular-shaped that would make a very nice stone bench. I left it propped up against a tree on the far bank a little bit upstream. Maybe next weekend I'll work on it.

Last year I was not that optimistic about the future of the six-foot-wide stream. Successive seasons of drought seemed to have depressed trout numbers—at least among larger fish. Persistent low water makes them particularly vulnerable to predators, especially birds. I saw large white jets of guano on certain rocks, indicating great blue herons had worked the stream over. This most recent summer has been wet and cool for the most part, and I've seen so many trout fingerlings happily swimming about that I have newfound hope.

But it does seem like the stream muddies easier now and doesn't run as clear as I remember during those first few years. I'm not sure if it's due to slumping streambanks that still haven't recovered from the floods or other factors at work.

I would love to start some sort of association of landowners along the stream. I could see organizing work days to stake more willows or plant seedlings and maybe eradicate the small patches of knotweed growing downstream. Maybe we could partner with a local Trout Unlimited chapter or some other group to build some in-stream structures to house more trout.

The downstream culvert pipe surely blocks some trout migration. It would be great to work with the town and have it repositioned. I do think the stream has the potential to be even more productive, both as a spawning tributary and as a haven for brook trout. More wild trout is never a bad thing. Unless you're a mayfly, I guess.

Next season, I'm thinking about trying more night fishing for trout on the Delaware. They say the biggest trout only come out at night. More importantly, there are fewer anglers to contend with. This year, the guide boats were really out of control. During May and June, it looked like the 6th Fleet descended on the river. As soon as one boat passed, two more came bearing down like attacking Viking longships. Unfortunately, guide boats make me fish like a schmuck. Take what happened recently: I had two trout working. One was within casting range, but the other was 50 yards downstream. My plan was to take my time and hopefully have shots at both fish—not too much to ask for. Along came a guide boat, so what did I do? I rushed my cast to fish number one, which immediately stopped rising; then I decided to wade as quickly as I could to the second fish. By the time I reached it, fish number one started rising again, just as the guide boat approached. Sure enough, it dropped anchor, and the sport began fishing so close to me, I could hear the flick of his cigarette lighter and shortly thereafter smelled his cigar. Then, instead of listening to singing warblers, I was forced to hear an infomercial about the newest $800 Sage rod (turns out the guide was a Sage rep). Adding insult to injury, the sport hooked fish number one, which turned out to be a fine 18-inch, two-pound male brown trout. I know this because I watched it get landed, weighed, measured, handed back and forth—oops, dropped it in the boat!—then photographed from a variety of angles, and finally released, probably as eel food. After the high-five, they pulled anchor and drifted so close to fish number two that they immediately spooked it. Thanks, guys.

Jealousy? Maybe a little for catching the fish. An accurate portrayal of what's happening more and more? Oh yeah. The river is a shared resource, I know that. With sharing should come courtesy. So how about giving the wade guys some space? As in, Why don't you try around the next bend? I hear there may be some risers two miles from here. Big fish. All yours. Go get 'em!

The glut of drift boats has put some landowners on edge about anglers walking the banks or even anchoring. Depending on which branch of which river, they have every legal right to kick people out. Again, this makes it tough for us wade guys who had been quietly fishing unofficial access points and turnoffs for years without any trouble but suddenly find ourselves facing new and adamant posted signs from a pissed-off landowner. And I don't blame them.

Back to night fishing: I tried it just once but randomly picked what had to be the brightest full moon I have ever seen up here.

Apparently, trout, like striped bass, shun a fat, cheesy moon. And while I will say it was a lovely experience casting into the river with the world around me bathed in blueish moonlight, I can report that I did receive a sound skunking.

If I do take it up, I'll have to hit the tying bench and crank out some giant Stimulators or something else that pushes water. Might need to upgrade to a beefier fly rod. I hear Sage has one that casts 200 feet.

But right now, I'm not going to worry about any of these things. Instead, I think I'll sit here on the porch and continue sipping this beer and look for the brookie that rises off the undercut bank. The door, the ceiling, the wall, the roof, the mice, the trees, even the fishing, can all wait.

It is, after all, a *cabin*.

-Fin-